MATBOARD Magic

Creative Matboard Craft Projects to Enhance Your Home

by Eileen L. Hull

Matboard Magic
by Eileen L. Hull

© 2008 Logan Graphic Products, Inc.,
Wauconda, IL
All rights reserved.
Printed in the United States of America
BookMasters, Inc.
Ashland, Ohio

ISBN 0-9749683-1-5

Credits

Photography: Rick Casarra

Design & Layout: Connie Miley Cook

Proofreading: Annalise Raziq

Project Design: Eileen L. Hull

About the Author

Photo courtesy of Hayward Hull

*Find a job you love
and you'll never work a day in your life.*

Confucius

Never was this quote more true than for professional crafter Eileen Hull. (Having raised four children while her husband was in the military, Eileen might argue this point.) However, her professional crafting career leaves many green with envy. Her ingenuity, resourcefulness and creativity have allowed her to make a career out of her hobby and passion–paper crafting.

Eileen is a freelance designer, specializing in three-dimensional artwork. She has owned and operated her own business, Paperwork, Etc. for twenty-five years. She continues to promote matboard crafts and recycling thrift store finds into new and useful items. Her work has appeared in magazines, including *Crafts 'n Things*, *PaperWorks*, *CardMaker* and *Creative Home Arts*. She has also contributed projects to other books, including *101 Paper-Craft Gift Ideas*, *Altered Art* and *Holiday Paper Fun*. She is a member of the Craft and Hobby Association, Washington Calligrapher's Guild, and Dulles Women's Networking Group.

Acknowledgements

Our sincere thanks to Crescent® Cardboard for generously donating all of the matboard used throughout this book.

My sincere thanks to:

Hayward
so glad I have you

all the folks at
Logan Graphic Products

Rick for the
great photography

my super creative friends
Kimberly
Lorine & Stephanie

my girls: Pam, Jess & Maryanne

for listening to me talk
about matboard :-)

Chris - we're so proud
of you. Glad you are home
safely from Iraq. Mom

the C.G.s
my encouraging friends

...and of course to all the crafters who find inspiration within these pages!

Eileen L. Hull

Keep it simple...
or challenge yourself!
Each featured project has a
difficulty and time indicator. Not
sure where your skills are? Start
easy and work up to more
challenging projects.

Time	Difficulty
3 hrs.	Advanced

Contents

Versatile and sturdy, matboard is the perfect material for 3-D craft projects like these. Use your own imagination for limitless possibilities!

Introduction

matboard- *(mat' boord)* n. 1. A heavy fiber, paper-like board used to protect artwork. It enhances and showcases the subject being framed and is usually acid free or pH treated. 2. A thick paperboard used to add dimension to framed artwork; available in a wide variety of colors and textures. 3. The most versatile paper ever created. 4. Provides a beautiful surface for stamping, stenciling, embossing and many other crafting techniques. 5. Can be used to create three-dimensional boxes, totes and books. 6. Looks great when embellished with glitter, metal, buttons, ribbon, chalks, ink, texture paste...

Come on, you know you've seen it around!
I am sure that everyone reading this book has some familiarity with matboard...perhaps you had your child's artwork immortalized under glass by a local craft shop, or you bought a pre-cut mat to display a collection of family photos. Surely everyone has had the pleasant experience of sitting at the dentist's office gazing at the matted artwork while waiting to be seen...the fact is, matboard is everywhere!

In my "Framing 101" class, we learned that the purpose of matting is to complement the artwork. Well, I believe it's time to look at this product with new eyes. There is no reason why a beautiful sheet of sturdy paper board like this should be used as a two-dimensional window to surround artwork, when IT can actually BE the artwork! With some fun tools and a piece of matboard, I will share my secret tricks of the trade with you on how to cut, score and decorate the matboard to create beautiful and unique three-dimensional pieces for you to share (or keep...)

TOP TEN REASONS TO LOVE MATBOARD:

10. It doesn't talk back

9. It's inexpensive

8. Comes in a huge assortment of colors and textures

7. Readily available

6. Large size means you can build large projects

5. Great weight for mailing

4. Too thick to give paper cuts

3. Old product used in a new way

2. The texture is just right for stamping

1. It's easy to score!

Where can I buy matboard?

Many of the large chain stores carry matboard, especially those with in- store matting and framing services. You can buy it by the sheet or have it cut to size (for a price!). The specialty mats are not always available at these stores but the basics are there.

Art supply stores usually carry a fairly extensive selection and what they don't have in stock, they can order for you.

Matting and framing studios are another source of matboard. I have had good luck working with some local shops. Many prints that they frame have large inside pieces that are cut from the middle of a mat (called fall-out). They reuse them when possible but most of the time, have to recycle or throw them out because they don't have room to store it all. I asked if I could buy some and we struck a deal. It helped the store owner because he didn't have to clear it out and was making money on something he would just have thrown out. I was happy to get a good price on a big selection of board. The downside to that is you don't necessarily get to choose what colors you get. You could always use board like that to practice on, or paint it and make it the color you want!

Another option is mail order. The prices and selection are good but shipping costs add up. As for me, I do buy through the mail and nothing makes me happier than seeing the delivery driver huffing and puffing up my path with a big old box of matboard!

With the huge photography and scrapbooking trends still on the upswing, I expect matboard's popularity to increase as people discover how easy it is to work with and how nice it is to have a custom matting studio in the comfort of your home.

Your matboard projects are only as great as the cutting tools you use. In this book, you will become familiar with the Logan mat cutting system. Instructions on straight and beveled cuts, how to score to the perfect depth for nice crisp folds and how to cut a single mat are included.

Above: Author Eileen Hull cutting a bevel mat using the Logan 301-S Compact Mat Cutter

Buying a mat cutter is a great investment. With what you would spend to mat and frame a picture in a custom frame shop, you can BUY the whole cutting system and have it to use on many projects to come. I can't tell you how many dollars I have saved by matting photos, artwork, cross stitch and many other projects myself. The tools are easy to use and well worth the small investment.

Here's how it all began...

I learned to use a mat cutter on a military post where family members had access to the arts and crafts center. At that time, I was doing a lot of cross stitch and couldn't afford to have everything matted and framed professionally. Having four small children at home, the center was sometimes a more enjoyable place to be than our house on bath night so I'd try and get over when I could. When we later moved to the Washington, DC area, the nearest arts and crafts center was 45 minutes away. That's when I realized I had gotten too used to having access to a mat cutter. I researched them and decided to take the plunge and buy one of my own. The purchase of my Logan 700 Simplex mat cutter was one of the best purchases I have ever made. I built a business around it, designing and selling matted artwork related to military life. After a while, my studio began to pile up with scraps of matboard too beautiful for the trash! The colors were so pretty–surely there had to be a use for it. I started to play around with it, cutting here, scoring and bending there. To my delight, three dimensional designs began to emerge. A little purse, a box to hold my magazines, a stationery folder... With a little glue, a rubber band strategically employed to hold things together and some fun embellishments, I had a great time making all kinds of boxes, books and totes.

Confession time

My name is Eileen Hull and I am a paper addict. My friend buys shoes, my sister buys fabric... well, I buy paper. The good (and bad) thing is it is widely available. Everywhere you look, there's paper. From the scrapbook stores to office supply outlets to drugstores to expensive boutiques, there is paper–ready, willing and waiting to be bought. Colors, textures, finishes, different shapes and patterns all combine to create a feast for your eyes and hands. And who knows when the urge to create will strike? A palette of paper is necessary to have on hand so that the projects can flow when they will.

So I buy paper, and my absolute favorite kind is matboard. Once you get your hands on a piece of this, you will never go back to chip board. In my opinion, matboard is the ultimate in paper because it is sturdy, smooth, available in many colors, fabrics and finishes, inexpensive and feels so substantial.

There are several different grades:

- **standard**—composed of processed wood pulp that will eventually discolor and break down. However, it easy to find and comes in a wide array of colors. For the purpose of the projects in this book, this is probably a very good choice for most designs.

- **conservation**—made of cotton or more purified wood pulp and lasts longer than the standard without breaking down.

- **rag**—museum quality board made from compressed cotton pulp. The most expensive and has the least variety, but will last a good long time without breaking down.

- The standard size sheet is 32" x 40", which allows you to create large pieces of artwork without any problem. Most boards are archival and "green," having been processed without harsh chemicals or additives. The cotton used to make it is an annually renewable resource.

- Chipboard is unsuitable for framing purposes because it is acidic and should not lay against the artwork. The texture is uneven and it is prone to fading.

I hope you will try these projects and go on to create your own beautiful works of art. Re-do a room in new colors! Make boxes to organize your desk, hold mail, store photos, or hold business cards. Sort your jewelry in a dresser caddy with removable bins and and store your pieces in a wall storage frame to hold necklaces and bracelets, as well as earrings and pins. Frames and stationery boxes make great gifts for everyone you know.

Every new couple would love to have a beautiful wedding keepsake created just for them. And what bride doesn't need a little organization with all the details to keep track of? A wedding guest book is a great way to start memories of married life together. But don't put it away in the closet after the wedding. Keep it in your entry hall and have visitors sign in. At Christmas, add pages and keep track of who you sent cards to.

Add some extra zip to your next holiday party when you set a table with this easy tree and packages centerpiece. Make a snowman and keep him out until the snow goes away. A box of cards is a great gift at any time of year.

Try your hand at cutting a beveled mat and frame your family photos.

In this book, you will learn how to make a wedding remembrance and guest book, place cards, jewelry box and organizers, photo frames, desk accessories, home décor for your holiday dinner table, card and gift boxes, and how to mat artwork. There are projects for all ages and interests to create. Take ideas from the pages in

the book and run with them to create 3-D boxes and books in your own colors and style. Embellish with supplies you already have on hand. Make them for your family and friends, for gifts, for special occasions or just for the fun of it.

As you go through the book, you will see that each project has been rated for skill level. Don't be put off by this–some of them are rated advanced just because of the time it takes to do them or the number of steps involved, not because they are exceptionally hard. You can do it. Give it a try today!

I would like to show you how I created the projects found in this book. Believe me, if there was a wrong way to do something, I did it. I'd like to spare you my mistakes and share the tips and techniques that I have learned along the way.

Get comfy on the couch, page through these beautiful projects and decide which one you want to try first! Any of these projects can be changed to reflect your personality, your colors, your style. Get started now! And most importantly, have fun... ❧

Tools and Techniques

I confess that this is the section of the book that I usually skip... and then wind up coming back to when I finally admit I can't figure it out on my own and need help. Whenever you read this, take your time and practice the techniques. A quality project is sure to follow!

Make sure you also read the complete and detailed instructions provided with your equipment. For more information on the products, visit the web sites of the manufacturers that are located in the Source section. The following is a brief overview of the tools and how they can be used.

Ideas for laying out your work space are also provided, as well as tools to keep on hand. As we all know, good tools can make or break the project.

Tools:

Logan 301-S Mat Cutter

This mat cutter is a workhorse. The best thing about it is the stable straight edge and measuring guide. Since my mat cutter is in the middle of my studio, I use it all the time for scoring, cutting, and trimming down stacks of paper, in addition to my mat cutting and construction projects.

This set is a great value and includes the cutting board, straight cutting head, bevel cutting head, slip sheet, blades and instructional DVD.

Cutting your board down to size is a breeze. Using the guide rail, place your straight cutting head into the track and pull toward you for perfectly straight 90–degree cuts in seconds. It's so much better using this than a mat knife–you get nice straight cuts in only one pass. Set the mat guide for board widths up to 4 ¼". If you need a wider piece, mark where you want to cut with ruler and T-square, remove the mat guide and hold the board steady with your left hand while cutting with the right.

To use the bevel cutting head, first mark the mat opening on the back side of the matboard. This

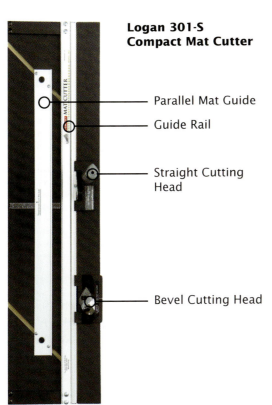

**Logan 301-S
Compact Mat Cutter**

— Parallel Mat Guide

— Guide Rail

— Straight Cutting Head

— Bevel Cutting Head

Designer Tip

Here's one of my favorite tricks! When scoring a stack of cardstock in half, adjust the mat guide for desired measurement (up to 4 ½") of scoring line. Butt the stack of cards up under the mat guide and against the guide rail. With an embossing stylus, press firmly against the side of the mat guide and score down the middle of the card. Before removing, bend the paper up to a 90–degree angle and finger press against the metal guide. Remove top card and repeat for the remainder of the stack. This method ensures quick, precise and sharp creases every time! ❧

can be done quickly and easily by setting the mat width on the parallel mat guide. Then just insert the matboard under the guide rail and up against the mat guide. Draw a pencil line along the length of the board, rotate the mat 90 degress and repeat for all sides. Next, hook the bevel cutting head onto the guide rail and align the start and stop indicator line with the pencil line closest to you. With your thumb, push the blade into the mat and slide the cutting head forward until the start and stop indicator reaches the upper pencil line. Retract the blade, rotate the board and repeat for the remaining sides.

Aligning the start and stop indicator using the bevel cutting head of the Logan 301-S Mat Cutting System

The size of this cutter is another advantage. All the projects in the book can be completed using this tool. Unless you are matting large pieces of art, you probably won't need anything bigger than 29". I recommend keeping it set up all the time and you will see how often you go over and use it. If you are challenged for space, it packs up into the box and stores easily.

Logan 500 Mat Knife

There are many versions of the "mat" or "craft" knife. For me, it comes down to comfort and what feels best in my hand. Many of the pencil-style knives with round

Logan 500 Mat Knife

barrels and very sharp tips work great for details and tight curves. However, I prefer the Logan mat knife for most projects in this book. The handle has a solid base that doesn't twist around in your hand and is very comfortable when scoring or cutting. The mat knife has a rounded corner under where the blade rests. I use that rounded part to rest on the board, slowly engaging the blade exactly where I want it and providing great control.

Logan 270 Blades

Blade changing is quick and easy on any Logan system. Make sure to change blades frequently. For a few cents per blade, it's worth having a fresh blade for perfect cuts.

An economical feature of the 270 blade is that it is the replacement blade for both the straight and bevel cutters, and also the mat knife. That means you can buy a pack of 100 and use the blades interchangeably with all of your tools. Plus, the blades are reversible so you get double the usage from each blade. It also is handy for trimming stubborn corners that won't pop out. Take the blade and slide it in the corner at the same angle it is cut at and gently continue the cut until the piece falls out.

Designer Tip

Recycle your blades! They are great for scraping windows after painting, getting into cracks to clean, scraping off stubborn price stickers, trimming caulk edges, and cutting articles and coupons out of the newspaper. Be careful though–they are very sharp! ❧

T-square

The T-square is very useful in squaring up edges to 90-degree angles. The "T" part of the tool lays along the edge of the board with the arm extending perpendicular down the length of the board. If the arm lines up with the rest of the board, you have a square corner. If not, use the arm to mark a straight line and then move to your mat cutter and trim off uneven edges.

Embossing Stylus

There are several versions of these tools available. This tool is used for scoring or dry embossing. The tip is used to press the outline of a stencil onto paper, thereby leaving a raised impression of the design on the other side.

The barrel may be made from wood, plastic or metal. Some are single-ended, some are double. The size of the tip varies from very fine to wide.

The Logan 4-Way Stylus is different because not only is it double-ended, but it has two extra tips included that store in the metal barrel. One of the tips is a metal piercing tool for use in pergamano, or paper piercing.

ATG Tape Gun

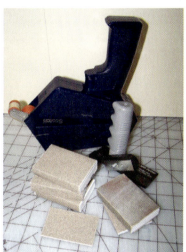

This tool is something I use every day of my life! The tape gun was designed for use in matting. It is a hand held double-sided tape dispenser.

I use it to wrap gifts, for card-making and other paper crafts, for use around the house, office and school. Probably the hardest thing to figure out is how to change the tape roll, and that's not too hard. I have given these as Christmas gifts to my favorite people over the years and they are now big fans too.

Sandpaper/Emery Board

These items are indispensible to have around your work space. The sandpaper is great for distressing matboard edges to give that shabby chic look. If you are working with a rough blade and have some tears after cutting, they are easily sanded down with sandpaper or an emery board. I use the sandpaper for larger projects and the emery board for fine or small areas. Keep a supply of coarse to fine papers in your studio. Both products are often available in the dollar stores.

Designer Tip

How to make a sanding block

Cut a long 2" strip of foam board with your straight cutter. Further cut down to 2" x 3" pieces. Stack together about 4-5 layers of foam board and tape together. With your tape gun, lay several lines of double-sided tape down on the block. Cut a piece of sandpaper to wrap around the block and trim excess paper. Magic! This is just the right size to hold in your hand and distress edges of matboard. Make several and use one each for dark, medium and light colors.

Pencil

Believe it or not, I have a favorite pencil! I use a mechanical pencil with the plastic barrel that comes with about nine lead refills inside. You simply rotate the lead for a nice sharp tip every time. And no messy sharpening!

Eraser

My preference in erasers is the kind that looks like a pen with a plastic barrel. The white eraser tip always does a great job of removing stray pencil lines, some scratches, smudges, chalks, and assorted messes. Refills are available for purchase–always a nice benefit...

Cork-Backed Metal Ruler

A good straightedge is a very important tool. Not only is it used for measuring, but the metal side provides a great guideline for scoring matboard and paper. The cork backing helps prevent the ruler from slipping when pressure is applied against it. Metal is good because it will stand up to the blade of the mat knife against it and not cut into it. Plastic and wood rulers are good for some things but when you are working with a sharp metal blade, it will cut them up in no time.

Self-Healing Mat

A large self-healing mat is kept under my work area and functions there very well. A self-healing mat stands up to a lot of abuse. The one I have is large–30" x 36", made of plastic and has 1" grid lines, which helps when checking for square corners. The best part is you can use your mat knife to trim board, a rotary cutter for fabric, or any other type of blade and the mat will not come apart or show damage.

Since my mat cutting area is probably the biggest open surface I have (when I don't have a bunch of unfinished projects sitting on it!), that is where I'll cut fabric using my rotary cutter, lay out designs, set eyelets, assemble parts, glue, cut, etc. When the mat gets dirty or full of fabric threads, I just take my bottle of glass cleaner, spray it down and wipe off. Then on to the next project!

Glue

There are so many glues out there, it's hard to figure out which to use for what! For the projects in this book, I am looking for certain qualities in a glue. I want a product that dries quickly and clear. One that is repositionable is a plus, so you can fix up those little accidents. A strong bond is also desired.

Beacon's Zip Dry Paper Glue is my favorite to use in working with dimensional matboard. It has all the qualities listed above. Experiment with what you have on hand and see what works best for you.

Glue Gun

Although I have been working with a glue gun for years, it still scares me a little. I have been burned countless times. The glue dries yellow and leaves all those strings everywhere. The tip is big and it's hard to get into tight spaces when working on some of the projects in the book. But there is no substitute for its staying power! Sometimes you need a very strong bond and that's what the glue gun provides. Consider using this if your project requires parts to be permanently attached.

Spray Adhesive

Spray adhesive is very handy when attaching two layers of paper together. I use it to adhere vellum to matboard or paper since it doesn't leave any marks like tape does. You can spray the back of a piece of scrapbook paper, lay it on matboard and then cut a mat. Voila! You will have a custom mat with perfect beveled edges in just the colors and design you want to surround your artwork.

Workable Fixative

This spray protects the surface you have been working on. Some mediums smudge and this prevents that from happening.

I address envelopes in calligraphy for my clients. Since some inks aren't permanent, I spray them with this after I've finished them. Using chalks for a soft accent are a favorite technique of mine, but often they rub off if not set. A quick spray of this works great. If you are using pigment ink on a stamping project, this product speeds the drying time. Overall, I like to use this on items that I know will be getting a lot of wear. With a barely wet sponge, you can wipe off fingerprints and marks from matboard after spraying with this without damaging the project.

Rubber Bands

Collect an assortment of sizes and widths. These are used to temporarily hold the sides of the boxes and designs together while the glue is setting.

Scrap matboard to practice on!

Please please **PLEASE** practice before you cut into the board you are using for your project. I guarantee you will be glad you did.

Above: Using rubber bands to hold a box together while the glue sets

Designer Tip

Gift wrapping goes so much faster when you get an assembly line going using your mat cutter. Line up the roll of wrapping paper to the size needed and just zip down the edge with your straight cutter–an even cut every time and no tearing like when you try that with scissors! Keep all other necessities close by–scissors tape, tags and pens. Soon the stack of beautifully wrapped gifts mounts quickly. 🐦

Techniques

To complete the projects in the following pages, some practice of new techniques and equipment may be required. They are not difficult but don't be discouraged if it doesn't come out perfectly the first time. It gets easier every time you do it... much like everything else in life...

STRAIGHT CUTTING

Using the Logan Mat Knife

Press knife straight down into board and run blade along line or ruler 2-3 times until you cut through matboard. Maintain steady pressure. Don't try to cut all the way through in one pass. NOTE: Use the Logan Mat Knife with the 301-S Mat Cutter (as shown) or with any suitable straight edge.

Using the Logan Straight Cutting Head

Place the groove of the cutting tool into the ridge running along the edge of the mat guide. Mark desired cutting lines on the wrong side.

Line up on the guide rail and pull cutter firmly toward you. With your left hand, hold the board so it doesn't shift while cutting.

SCORING

Measure board and mark desired scoring lines in pencil. Press mat knife down firmly (but not TOO firmly) and go over scoring line once or twice with even pressure. The goal is to cut a little more than halfway through the board. It is better to be tentative at first until you get the hang of this. The board should bend cleanly and without too much pressure. As you experiment, you will get the feel of the board. However, when cutting different textures and finishes, make sure to always cut a practice piece first since some of the specialized matboards are thicker and take more passes to score cleanly.

Above: A bevel cut mat created using the Logan 301-S Mat Cutting System

BEVEL CUTTING

How to cut a single beveled mat:

Always place a slip sheet of scrap matboard on the cutting board and underneath the mat you are cutting to stabilize the blade.

Place the board to be cut under the guide rail and on top of the backing sheet. Set the mat guide to the desired width and tighten knobs.

Measure and mark your cutting lines on the back side of the matboard. Turn the mat on all four sides and draw a line down the side where the cut should go making sure to show where lines intersect.

With the blade retracted, set the bevel cutter into the guide rail. Line up the white line seen on the right side of the cutter with the measurements penciled on the back of the mat. Ease the blade into the board.

Push the cutter forward to make a smooth and even bevel cut. Retract the blade when the white line and end point meet.

Repeat on all four sides. The inside window should just pop out when the fourth side is cut.

Designer Tip

When matting a project with asymmetrical windows, remember that the openings that you pencil on the back of the mat will be the reverse from what you see on the front when you cut it.

Because I have made this mistake so many times, I have devised a way to prevent it. I cut the shape of each window from a piece of paper and spray with a light coat of spray adhesive. I lay the paper windows (adhesive side on top) on scrap mat the size of the mat I am cutting and arrange to my liking. When everything is in position, I take the mat I am cutting and place the back side on top of the arrangement. The spray adhesive allows the paper to stick in place and I know which way it's supposed to go. I can mark the windows and know that they are going to wind up where they are supposed to. It is a little extra work but beats messing up a mat!

For more information on mat cutting...

Take a trip to the library and take out some books on the subject. There are very cool cuts and styles to be explored here, as well as tips on proportion and color. Learn what your equipment can do for you and try some new ideas. See page 72 for other Logan books on mat cutting and framing.

MORE TIPS

Always use a sharp new blade. Be very careful when cutting. ***These projects are not recommended for children under 16.*** Make sure you measure, mark and cut very carefully. Even being 1/16th of an inch off can mess up the whole design. Before cutting/scoring on the project, make sure to practice on a scrap of matboard. If you have not scored deeply enough, it will be difficult to bend. Take your knife and go over your line again. If you have scored too deeply, you may have cut through the board. Lucky you are using your practice piece! If you do make a mistake and cut all the way through the board, you can patch with clear

bandage tape from the inside before assembling!

DAMAGE CONTROL:

- If you have not scored through the board deeply enough, it will be difficult to bend. Take your knife and go over your line again.

- If you have scored too deeply, you may have cut through the board. If so, patch with clear bandage tape from the inside before assembling. Even if you chop a side off, all is not lost!

- Ragged edges are eliminated by inserting a fresh blade.

- If corners don't meet, your angle may be a little off. The next time you cut, make sure the matboard is square using a t-square.

- If paper is separating from the board when you try to bend it, then it's not scored deeply enough.

- If the project is bending in the opposite direction than you want, it means you scored the board on the wrong side.

- Ragged edges? Use an emery board or sandpaper to file down.

- Use a razor blade to trim bevel corners that are not quite cut all the way through.

- Suede, linen, denim and fabric mats may be likely to fray. Use a razor blade to trim stray threads.

SETTING UP YOUR WORKSPACE

My mat cutter is set up in my studio all the time, ready and waiting for any mat cutting emergency. It sets on two dressers of the same height and rests on a tabletop placed on the dressers. Under the tabletop and in between the dressers I store my matboard. It stands up and is sorted by color. I use the boxes they come in to hold each color. Although this works fairly well, I am always looking for a better way to protect the board from moisture and warping. My studio is in the basement so I keep a dehumidifier going nearby.

The dresser drawers are used to hold supplies: spare blades, tape for the ATG gun, framing points, etc. The table is large enough to accommodate a whole sheet of matboard. A big self-healing mat with a grid lays on the work area. A yardstick and T-square are hanging on the side of the dresser. My tape gun is close at hand.

Initially, I had a problem with my mat cutter slipping a little on the slick table surface. I took a piece of foam shelf liner and adhered it to the base of the cutter and now it stays perfectly in place with no slipping!

I found early on that it's easier on the back to raise the height of the equipment to about 38" off the ground, which is a little higher than most tables. Of course, it depends on how tall you are. Just make sure you are comfortable.

VOCABULARY

Archival—a material having a neutral or slightly alkaline pH; it should also have good aging properties.

Backing board—board that supports artwork behind a window mat.

Fall-out—piece of matboard that "falls out" of the window when a mat is cut

Flaw board—board that is dented, scratched or flawed in manufacturing. Often used for backing or as a slip sheet.

Overcut—this happens when you don't end the cut where you should.

Rabbet—edge on the back of the frame where artwork is inserted

Right side—the colored or patterned side of the board

Score—cut with a sharp blade about halfway through the matboard. The object of scoring is to weaken the fibers of the board so it bends in half

Slip Sheet—scrap matboard that is placed under matboard that is being cut, for both bevel and straight cutting. The slip sheet protects table surfaces as well as preserves the cutting blade

Window- opening cut into mat

Wrong side- back of matboard, usually white

BASIC BOX CONSTRUCTION

Determine the size of desired box, including height, width and depth. Draw a rough sketch,

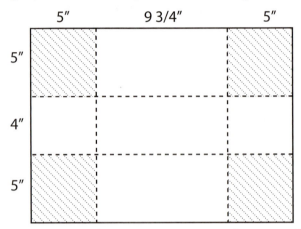

inserting your dimensions, on graph paper. Draw dotted lines or use another color to designate lines to be scored.

Following the pattern, lightly pencil your cutting and scoring lines on the right side of the matboard. After scoring, test your cuts by folding them to a 90-degree angle. Turn the board over to the wrong side. You should see where you have scored by a fold line. Cover these scoring lines using clear tape. This will reinforce your seams and strengthen your box.

After you have finished with all cutting and scoring, assemble the box. If you are going to add eyelets, punch holes, cut slits, stencil, stamp, paint or anything else, do this work while the box is flat. Erase any pencil lines with a white eraser. Hold box together with a rubber band. Using Zip Dry Paper Glue, reinforce corners with lines of glue for an extra strong

box. Let set for 30 minutes. Embellish the box as you desire!

BE CREATIVE!

- Add embellishments of all kinds—papers, fibers, fabric, ribbon, eyelets, brads, metal.

- Matboard can be distressed by rubbing with sandpaper or emery board.

- You can use a brass stencil and press image into matboard with a stylus, then dry brush over image with stamp pad ink on stencil brush for a soft effect. Mat can be painted, textured and stenciled.

- You can decoupage paper over it, inside it, cover with fabric, or use it to tie up the box.

- Use rubber bands for closures, buttons, rivets or brads.

- Use the squares you have cut from corners as tiles to accent the box with letters and words or save them for another project.

- Stamp on matboard to personalize or customize.

- Apply appliqués, crystals or glitter to sparkle up a box.

- Monograms are huge. Add stickers, stencils or stamps to any project to make it more personalized.

- Working on a large project and need paper larger than standard scrapbooking paper? Use good quality gift wrap or wallpaper instead.

LITTLE KNOWN MAT FACTS:

- Matboard can be cut with scissors (but a professional mat cutting tool is easier and more precise!).

- You can use hole punches that don't have a lot of angles (round are best).

- You can stencil on suede for a beautifully shaded effect.

- If you have a color board you don't like, paint it!

Get creative with embellishments! Beads, buttons, glitter, sequins, lace, ribbons, stencils, etc. make great enhancements.

- Want white? Use the back side of the board.

- You are working with the most versatile paper product of the century!

Gluing Choices

There several factors that will affect the type of glue you will use in a project. One is how the design will be used. Is it a box that will be opened over and over again? Is it a design that will remain in place once set?

I like Zip Dry Paper Glue by Beacon. It dries clearly and quickly. If you get more on the project than you want, you can rub it off like rubber cement. It won't leave dirty marks or tear the paper.

For heavy duty jobs, I recommend using a glue gun. You have to work fast but the glue does hold very well. Sometimes I use the Zip Dry first to position the board and then when that dries and everything is in place, I use the glue gun on top of it.

If you need to glue large areas or adhere two sheets of paper or fabric together, the best choice would probably be spray adhesive. If you make a mistake, you can still lift up and reposition if you do it right away.

Say it with Stripes and Stamps

Cutting and scoring techniques are the focus of this chapter. These featured techniques add a lot of pizzazz to the desk set, yet are easy to do. The blotter is composed of a single sheet of matboard set in the middle and two striped borders going down each side. The slightly "off kilter" stripes going down the sides are created by a cutting and stacking technique, and are made in assembly line fashion. The pencil and tool caddies are pieces of decorated matboard wrapped around recycled soup cans. The wrap effect is achieved by scoring every ½" to allow the matboard to bend around the can. This technique can be used with other shapes also. The note holder is a basic box. You will see this shape everywhere you look—whether it's packaging, storage, décor or fun. Now you will be able to make your own boxes in whatever colors and dimensions you'd like!

The craft technique used to accent the desk set is rubber stamping. Stamps and inks work beautifully on the matboard surface. Watermark ink is a great way to get the look of subtle texture. To me, it is magic to watch the image emerge after stamping the design with this clear pad. The design comes out a little bit darker than the paper, whatever color the background may be. It gives a very soft effect that is great for backgrounds and creating some texture on plain paper. Magic. I'm telling you. ❧

In a world where computers are our main source of written communication, sometimes it's nice to sit down, take pen in hand and compose a handwritten letter. When the mood strikes to write, nothing sets the stage better than a pretty, well-organized desk. The desk set in this chapter is sure to inspire great correspondence. The pink and brown colors set a quiet and reflective mood. If you have to watch your balance dwindle while paying bills, at least you'll have something nice to look at...

Time	Difficulty
~3 hrs.	Advanced

Project:

Desk Blotter with Random Stripes

Technique: Striping

You will need:

- Crescent #1644 - Azalea
- Crescent #1097 - Fudge
- Logan 301-S Compact Mat Cutter with straight cutting head
- 4-5 coordinating flower rubber stamps- small to medium sizes
- Watermark stamp pad
- 2 coordinating ribbons – narrow and medium widths
- Freezer paper
- Clear adhesive tape
- Double-sided tape
- Logan Mat Knife
- Contact paper – 20" x 20"
- Digital photo & paper protectant spray

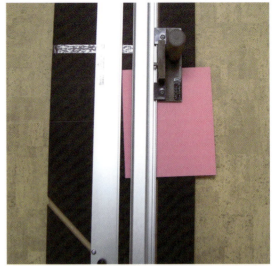

Above: Randomly sized strips are created by cutting matboard strips at an angle.

Stripes:

1. Cut two lengths of pink and brown strips of matboard, each measuring 1 ½" wide x 32" long. Divide 32" length into four 8" strips. You should have eight strips of each color, measuring 1 1/2" x 8".

Diagram 1

2. Place the narrow end of the strip at the top of the mat cutter, and set at a very slight angle. (Diagram 1) With mat knife, cut off a very small triangular strip (1/2" or less). The long sides should NOT be parallel. Cut each strip in a similar manner.

3. Cut a piece of freezer paper about 10" x 20". Lay three or four lines of double-sided tape down the 20" length of freezer paper. Lay the matboard strips in a column over the tape lines, alternating colors and keeping the edges tightly butted together. (Diagram 2) Press the strips down firmly when you have an arrangement that pleases you. You should have a long row of pink and brown randomly sized stripes adhered to the freezer paper.

Diagram 2

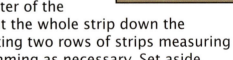

4. Mark the center of the stripe and cut the whole strip down the middle, creating two rows of strips measuring 16" x 3", trimming as necessary. Set aside.

Blotter middle:

1. Cut a piece of matboard that is 16" x 18". (Read **Maximizing Your Mat!** tips before cutting).

2. With stamps and watermark ink, randomly stamp around the edges. Allow to dry for 20- 30 minutes.

Assembly:

1. Take the two strips of pink and brown stripes and place them on either side of the large blotter piece. Turn all pieces over and rearrange them so all edges are tightly butted together. Temporarily secure with scotch tape.

2. Carefully cover entire back of blotter with contact paper, smoothing it down flat as you go. Trim edges with mat knife. Turn blotter over to right side.

3. Spray top of blotter with several coats of protectant spray to protect it from spills, dirt and oils. Allow to dry.

4. Cut two pieces of ribbon 18" long. Cover the seams where the boards meet with ribbon. Secure ends of ribbon to the back of the blotter.

Something Extra:

With a ¼" hole punch, punch pink and white circles from scrap paper. Dot them with glue and add randomly in the middle of the flowers to give a little extra dimension. 🐦

Designer Tip

Add any accents that you may wish to make this a beautiful and unique place to write a letter. Just remember to keep the surface fairly flat or you may be writing over some speed bumps! You may want to cut another layer of matboard and adhere it under the decorated top layer to anchor all sections together. 🐦

Additional Ideas

Now that you know how to make slightly off kilter stripes, regular straight ones should be a piece of cake! Repeat all steps as you did with the random stripes and eliminate the step of shaving off the small thin triangle. You should have 1 ½" rectangular strips that line up in a neat, straight row. Line up 6 alternating rows and cut down further into 1 ½" strips, creating a checkerboard effect. (Diagram 3) Arrange these as desired for a different border effect. ◈

Diagram 3

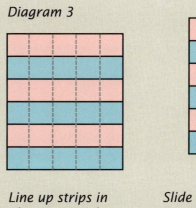

Line up strips in alternating colors and cut as shown.

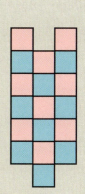

Slide the strips to create a checkerboard pattern

Time	Difficulty
1 hr.	Intermediate

Project:
Curvy Can Wraps
Technique: Wrapping Around Curves

You will need:

- Crescent #1644 - Azalea
- Crescent #1097 - Fudge
- Logan 301-S Compact Mat Cutter
- 2 tin cans – small and medium sizes
- Tape measure
- Logan Mat Knife
- Ruler
- Pencil
- Rubber stamps
- Watermark stamp pad
- Strips of pink and brown paper scraps
- 2 lengths of coordinating ribbons – narrow and medium widths
- Double stick tape
- Digital photo & paper protectant spray
- T-square

Designer's Tip

When covering a container, consider the size of the item and width of the scoring marks. If you are covering a large container, you may decide to score every 1". A wider circumference creates a gentler curve so you will not need to score as closely as for a smaller container. On a tall skinny vase, you might want to increase the frequency of scores to every ¼". When choosing a container to wrap, make sure the walls are all parallel. Slanted or angled containers will not work with this technique. ❧

1. With a tape measure, measure the circumference and height of each can. Cut matboard to exact size.

2. With stamps and ink, randomly stamp front of matboard on colored (right) side. Let dry 20 minutes.

3. On the right side of your board, measure and mark lightly in pencil every ½". Take the piece of board and place on your mat cutter. Using a T-square as a guide to keep your lines parallel, position pencil mark along cutting edge. With your mat knife, lightly score on line until blade cuts through board about halfway (see **Tools and Techniques** chapter). Repeat cut on remaining lines.

4. Spray board with protectant spray to protect against scuffing or moisture.

5. Wrap scored board around can and trim any excess. Apply double-sided tape on wrong side about every 3", making to sure include all edges. Press firmly around can and press to secure.

6. Measure around can and cut a strip of coordinating paper to size, adding 1" extra length for overlap. Place band around can and adhere with tape. On top of paper band, tie ribbon in knot and trim edges. Repeat with other can.

Additional Ideas

These can wraps are quick and easy to make. Cans and jars can be covered and coordinated for use all around the house. In my studio, I use mason jars to hold my paintbrushes, scissors, rulers, colored pencils and markers. They look so pretty lined up that I am inspired to craft!

For entertaining, I purchased a case of round mason jars. When I host an event, I make sleeves for them (like little slipcovers!) to match the theme of the party. Instead of taping them directly to the glass, they are secured inside the sleeve with tape so they are easy to slide on and off. The jar can then be filled with flowers, plants, flags, pinwheels, candles or other items to coordinate with the occasion, and used as centerpieces.

Give one to a friend with flowers from your garden to brighten her day. Stamp a message and her name on the sleeve to personalize. For a dinner party, use the jar with a single flower as a unique place card. Make a candle wrap for a wedding reception with the bride and groom's names hanging from a tag and embellish with pearls. ◈

Designer's Tip

One of the many wonderful qualities of matboard is that there is no fraying, seam allowances or unfinished edges to worry about. You can cut exactly what you measure. However, when working on a large piece, I usually do allow for a little extra board just to be safe. Trimming down afterwards is not a big deal and it's better to have too much than too little. 🐦

Maximizing Your Mat!

Matboard is sold by the sheet. A regular sheet measures 32" x 40". When working on projects that involve large pieces of board, try to figure out the best way to cut your matboard. Sit down with a calculator or sheet of graph paper and calculate where to make cuts that will produce the least waste. Not only is it very irritating to find hat you have cut a piece the wrong size, but if you have made a mistake in your initial layout, you may not have enough board left to complete your project. And that's <u>really</u> irritating!

For example, let's look at the blotter project. The measurements for the large middle piece are 16" x 18". Since a sheet of matboard is 32" wide, the number 16 should ring a bell! 16 is half of 32! We know that we can get 2 pieces from that 32" if we cut 18" from the long side of the board and 16" going up. That means we need to make a lengthwise cut on our full sheet at 18". That leaves a piece 18" x 32". This is cut in half again and leaves 2 pieces, each measuring 16" x 18". (Diagram 4) Of course it does not always work out exactly, but a good general rule is to leave the biggest possible piece of the sheet that you can. 🐦

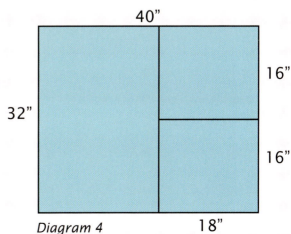

Diagram 4

Time	Difficulty
1 hr.	Easy

Project:
Memo Holder

Technique: Basic Open Box Construction

You will need:

- Matboard in pink or brown
- Logan 301-S Compact Mat Cutter
- Logan 500 Mat Knife
- Square memo pad
- Rubber stamps
- Watermark ink
- Ribbon
- Paper glue
- Rubber band
- Digital photo & paper protectant spray

1. Measure length, width and height of memo pad you wish to make a box for. Sketch out the dimensions on graph paper and draw a pattern. First, mark the bottom of the box in the middle of the page (Diagram 5). Then add the height and width of each side. The corner squares will be cut off as the box comes together.

Diagram 5

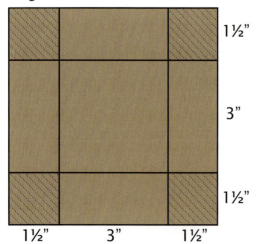

1½"

3"

1½"

1½"   3"   1½"

2. After the diagram is sketched, you may want to lay the memo pad on top of the pattern just to double check that you have measured correctly. Cut matboard to size of outer dimensions.

3. With rubber stamps and watermark ink pad, stamp randomly around the edge of the square. Spray with sealer to protect the box.

4. Referring to the sketch, mark scoring lines on the front of the matboard. Lay the board on the mat cutter, right (colored) side up, and use the guide on the top perpendicular bar to line up each side in the same position. This will ensure that all sides are exactly the same size. Cut the corner blocks away with the mat knife.

5. Fold the sides of the box upright. Wrap ribbon around the outside of the box to estimate how much ribbon you will need. Allow a little extra for the knot and cut.

6. Take both ends of the ribbon and wrap around the outside back of the box. Thread ribbon inside the 2 sides and back out the front of the box. Both ends should meet in the front. Tie in a knot and trim edges.

7. With paper glue, adhere all corners inside the box, laying a fairly thick coat over corners and ribbon. Wrap a rubber band around the outside of the box to keep the shape. Allow to dry for 20 minutes.

8. With watermark ink pad, stamp initial on memo sheets to personalize. Insert memo pad.

Additional Ideas!

Make extra boxes in various sizes and colors to hold different desk accessories—paper clips, rubber bands, business cards, binder clips, pre-inked stamps, address labels, postage stamps, etc. These could all be lined up at the top of the blotter close at hand. These boxes are also great for holding rings and earrings. Make a set to match your bedroom. This box is also a great addition at parties to hold small favors or candies. Use at each guest's place and write their name on the box to serve as a place card. These boxes are so quick and easy to assemble, you could make a set and use to organize your junk drawer—everyone has one of those! Separate all those little items you know you will need someday...

This box is quite versatile and once you make a few, you will be looking for reasons to make more! They can be embellished in so many other ways. ◈

Use the basic open box construction technique to make a cute basket like the one shown below.

Designer's Tip

It takes a while to train your brain to think "3-D." That's why I am a big fan of sketching. When everything is laid out on paper, I can see if there is an obvious mistake. It also helps, when calculating measurements, to see each piece in perspective. It is very important to measure, cut and score very consistently. It makes a difference when the final pieces have to be aligned. If you are 1/16th of an inch off, mistakes in cutting will show. 🐛

Dress Up Your Dresser!

Beautiful jewelry looks even better when stored in attractive containers. The soft green embossed suede matboard used in these projects coordinates with a purple print fabric and ribbon to allow the jewelry to be seen and selected easily, but is also attractive in its own right. The jewelry box contains several removable boxes sized to hold various treasured pieces. Putting earrings, bracelets and necklaces away after a hard day's work takes no time at all with the wall caddy. The photo frame that completes the set is a great accent and is very quick and easy to make.

Project:

Jewelry Box

Time	Difficulty
~3 hrs.	Advanced

Technique: Working With Fabric and Ribbon

Fabric and matboard are a great combination. The matboard provides a sturdy base on which to attach the fabric. The fabric softens the board and adds fun color and dimension to projects. Add some ribbon for more color. Use the ribbon as closures and accents and you have a winning design!

Fabric may be torn into strips, stapled to the back of a frame and used to hang artwork or glued to the back of a plate for hanging. Wrap fabric or ribbon around boxes and knot in the front. This provides extra support and a nice finishing touch to the box.

Something to keep in mind is that fabric does fray. To keep strings from getting out of control, take a dab of glue on the end of your finger and run it along any seams or corners where the fabric may stick out. The glue will prevent those annoying threads from getting in the way.

These projects make great gifts! You can dress them up or down by embellishing with your leftover scrapbooking supplies.

You will need:

- Logan 301-S Compact Mat Cutter
- Logan 500 Mat Knife
- Crescent # 9713428 Asparagus Foliage embossed matboard
- Crescent # 9560 Easter Egg matboard
- Glue
- Double-sided tape
- 1 yard coordinating cotton print fabric (a small, allover print is best—stripes or checks may be more difficult to line up)
- Spray adhesive
- 1/8" hole punch
- Tape gun
- Vellum
- Large decorative button with shank
- Ribbon
- Foam tape strips

Instructions:

CUT embossed asparagus foliage matboard:

- 13 1/4" x 22 1/4"

1. Mark off scoring lines of jewelry box lightly on the RIGHT side of the board. (Diagram 1)

2. Score matboard on RIGHT side referring to pattern and techniques in Designer Tips. Bend and fold box to make sure seams align and that all scoring lines have been cut enough to bend cleanly.

3. Iron fabric. Trim to cover jewelry box pattern plus 1" extra all around.

4. Lay a row of double-sided tape all around the edges of the box. Over tape, apply a layer of spray adhesive to the WRONG side of jewelry box.

5. Lay fabric over matboard WRONG sides together. Smooth fabric over mat.

Diagram 1

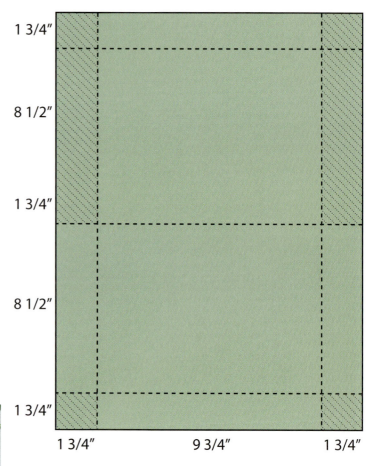

1 3/4"

8 1/2"

1 3/4"

8 1/2"

1 3/4"

1 3/4"   9 3/4"   1 3/4"

Designer's Tip

When working with suede or fabric matboard, be aware that the top layer of the matboard is thicker than regular matboard. You will either have to press harder or make more passes with the mat knife than you do with regular board to totally cut or score the board. Also, when working with an embossed board and a regular board, keep in mind that they are 2 different thicknesses, so measurements must be adjusted accordingly.

Another item to remember is that suede matboard does not adhere well to itself due to the nap of the fabric covering. If you need to glue it, use a heavy-duty glue or all-purpose glue.

The jewelry box is somewhat time-consuming but by the time you finish it, you'll be able to make an open box in your sleep! 🐰

6. Place box fabric side down on cutting mat. Trim edges of fabric with mat knife or rotary cutter.

7. On front bottom flap, take button and mark position of shank. Make sure that the shank is going up and down. With a ¼" hole punch, punch through matboard and fabric. Place button in hole, feeding the button shank to the inside of the box. Trim a very slim scrap of matboard and secure the shank on the back by threading it through. Glue mat scrap to fabric on inside of box, leaving a little space between button and box lid to accommodate flap.

8. On top front flap, mark position of shank hole and punch out. With mat knife, cut a notch from hole down to bottom of flap. The width of the notch should be wide enough to accommodate the button shank. The notch will slip into the button shank to close box securely.

9. Fold matboard up into box shape. Dab a small amount of glue over the fabric lining around the top edge of the box to prevent unwanted threads from sticking up.

10. Cut a 20" length of wide ribbon, wrap around lid and knot in front.

11. Embellish further as desired.

Inset: Score the box from the back side to make boxes.

Above: Fabric applied to the wrong side of the matboard.

Jewelry Box Inserts

Cut:

- Small Green Box: 2 pc. 5" x 5"
- Large Green Box: 1 pc. 3 ½" x 9 ½"
- Small Purple Box: 2 pc. 5" x 5"
- Medium Purple Box: 2 pc. 2 ¼" x 4 ½"

SMALL BOX:

1. Score the jewelry box on the WRONG (white) sides of board so the color is on the inside of box. (See Diagram 2)

2. Trim off the corners with mat knife.

Diagram 2

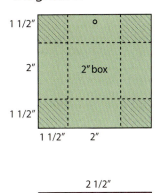

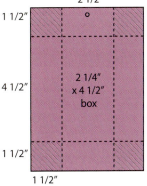

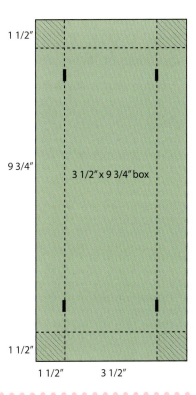

3. Cut a small scrap of ribbon (1 ½") and fold in half. Place both ends of ribbon centered near top on inside of box. Punch small hole through all 3 layers. Insert brad or eyelet to secure.

4. Fold up into box shape. Wrap with rubber band to keep in place while gluing.

5. Glue box where corners meet. Set aside to dry, keeping rubber bands in place.

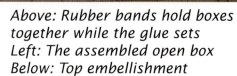

MEDIUM BOX:

1. Follow same directions as small box.

LARGE BOX:

1. Follow above to Step 2. Mark two slits on long sides of the box, each 1 ¼" from the end of the box. Ribbon will be slipped through to hold necklaces in place. Cut slits with craft knife. Cut two 8" lengths of ribbon. Thread from back to front of box and tie in knot.

2. Fold up into box shape. Wrap with rubber band to keep in place while gluing.

3. Glue box where corners meet. Set aside to dry, keeping rubber bands in place.

Above: Rubber bands hold boxes together while the glue sets
Left: The assembled open box
Below: Top embellishment

TOP EMBELLISHMENT:

CUT Green matboard with outer dimensions:

- 4" x 6"

1. Mark a 1" border all around. Following directions for cutting a beveled mat in Chapter 1 (p. 16), cut a 2" x 4" window. Trim ½" off each side of mat, creating a smaller border. (Diagram 3)

2. On the computer, lay out a label/title/verse in a 2" x 4" text box. Print out on vellum.

Diagram 3

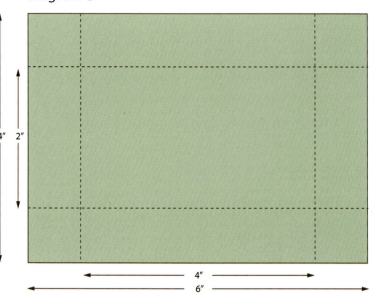

3. Lay a line of glue on the back of the small mat. Center thin mat over printed vellum label and press into place. Let vellum extend beyond the mat. Trim evenly with a small border of vellum showing.

4. Turn mat over. Put a line of foam tape all around the bottom of the mat and peel off adhesive backing.

5. Cut a 5 ½" x 3 ½" solid piece of scrap mat for background. With tape gun, tape edges of mat and criss-cross in the middle.

6. Cut a piece of fabric 6 ½" x 4 ½". Center fabric on scrap mat. Smooth and press down. Turn mat over and lay another line of tape around all edges. Wrap excess fabric around back and press into tape.

7. Turn piece over. This is the base for the small matted frame.

8. Position mat piece over fabric and adhere foam backing to fabric backing.

9. Center entire piece on main jewelry box.

Technique: Thin Mats

When you want to cut a mat thinner than 7/8", there are two ways to do it. Write the inner dimensions you want and add 2" to each side. Cut a piece of board to size, mark a 1" border and cut your beveled window. Don't worry that it's too big.

Plan A: You can trim 1" off each side leaving you with a 3" x 5" mat that's ½" wide!

Plan B: The other way to achieve this is to cut another mat inside the one you've already cut. After you cut your original window, simply move the mat another ½" down on the mat cutter and make a pencil mark.

Cut another beveled mat and you will now have 2 mats: the smaller inner one with a thin mat that you originally wanted and then one a little larger. What a deal!

Designer's Tip

I am a big fan of my tape gun. I use it often in place of, or in conjunction with, spray adhesive. I don't like to wait at all. The tape gun instantly dispenses double-sided tape, providing a fairly strong and quick bond. I first purchased mine for use in matting. It has become my favorite tool to give my crafting friends and family. It's great for adhering items when card-making, matting, working on scrapbook pages, three-dimensional projects, and photos. ❧

Additional Ideas!

Besides a jewelry box, this beautiful organizer can be used to store small craft items, buttons, beads, pins, coins, mementos, or pressed flowers. Customize your box sizes to fit items you'd like to store in this pretty place. Use ribbon loops to remove drawers from box. This would make a great pen case for the calligrapher. The pens could be stored in the long drawer and ink cartridges, nibs and erasers could each have their own tiny box. Colors can be coordinated as a gift for that special person for any occasion: wedding, Mother's Day, birthday, or just thinking of you. ◈

Thanks for everything, Mom. You're the best. Happy Mother's Day!

Love from your firstborn

Maureen

...and favorite child :-)

Thanks for everything, Mom. You're the best. Happy Mother's Day!

Project:
Frame Wall Caddy

Time	Difficulty
~2 hrs.~	Intermediate

You will need:

- Frame without glass – 11" x 14" (flat back preferable)
- Foam core to cover back of frame
- Crescent # 9713428 Asparagus Foliage embossed matboard
- Fabric to match matboard—1/2 yd
- Spray paint
- Spray adhesive
- Mat knife
- Straight cutter
- Oval mirror
- Brads
- 1/8" and 1/16" hole punches
- Graph paper
- Upholstery and thumb tacks
- Logan 4-Way Stylus

MEASURE:

   back of frame inset

   back of frame

CUT:

- foam core to cover entire back of frame
- 2 mat strips to go across short side of frame 1 ½" wide x width plus 1"
- 1 mat piece for corner (see Diagram 4)

Diagram 4

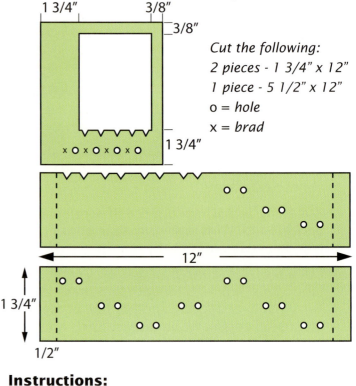

Cut the following:
2 pieces - 1 3/4" x 12"
1 piece - 5 1/2" x 12"
o = hole
x = brad

Instructions:

1. Spray frame in desired color. When dry, sand off paint randomly for a distressed look.

2. With straight cutter, cut a piece of foam core to fit back of frame.

3. Press fabric.

4. Apply heavy coat of spray adhesive to one side of foam core.

5. Lay fabric over foam core and smooth out bubbles and wrinkles.

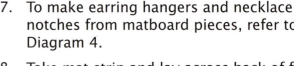

6. Lay foam piece fabric side down on self healing mat and trim fabric edges using the mat knife or rotary cutter.

7. To make earring hangers and necklace notches from matboard pieces, refer to Diagram 4.

8. Take mat strip and lay across back of frame. Make a pencil mark where mat lines up with

lip of frame. Add ½" to each side and trim. Score on RIGHT side of mat where strip will lay in frame and fold ½" remaining strip behind.

9. On WRONG side of strip, mark off every ½" on top left side for 4". Make notches with 1/8" hole punch for hanging necklaces. (Diagram 4)

10. Cut a piece of ¼" graph paper and place over the front of the strip. With the Logan 4-Way Stylus piercing tip, mark off holes as seen in pattern. Punch holes out with 1/16" hole punch.

11. Repeat for other strip.

12. Cut six 1 ½" foam core squares. Tape them together and place in the lower left corner of the large corner mat for support. Secure with glue or double–sided tape to the back of the mat. The height will depend on the depth of the frame you select so you may need more or less than 6 pieces.

13. Turn frame over and position strips and mat in place. Secure in place with a staple gun or thumb tacks. Refer to photo for placement. Include stack of foam core in corner.

14. Place mirror on fabric covered foam backing where desired. Mark 2 holes on top for ribbon placement. Poke holes through fabric and foam core with embossing stylus tool. Thread ribbon through holes and tie on top.

15. Center foam core backing over frame. Tack in place with upholstery tacks and hammer.

16. Add ribbon hanger to back, tacking in place.

Designer's Tip

Always be on the lookout in thrift stores for frames without glass. They are often of nice quality and priced very inexpensively. I always check frames for certain things. Here are my do's and don'ts:

- Only buy real wood frames—the plastic/ composite ones do not hold up well.

- Small nicks and dents are acceptable because I usually spray paint mine and distress them in some way, so a little flaw will not even be noticed. If you are using the frame for a more formal project and DO mind dents, sometimes they can be sanded or puttied and then spray painted.

- Check to make sure the corners are square and tight. ✿

Additional Ideas!

Use these frames to make a mosaic serving tray. Paint one in your child's school colors and use as a rotating gallery for your child's artwork. Insert foam core and cover with fabric and you have a custom bulletin board. Mat and frame a collection of old silver plated spoons and hang in the kitchen. For a dramatic display, spray paint a group of frames in cool colors and hang without artwork in them. ◈

Project:

Matboard Photo Frame

Time	Difficulty
 30 min.	Easy

You will need:

- Crescent # 9713428 Asparagus Foliage embossed matboard
- Bevel cutter
- Mat knife
- Tape gun
- Ribbon – 15" length
- Fabric 7" x 7"

Instructions:

CUT from embossed green:

- 12" x 6"
- 5 ½" x 6"

FRAME

1. Score large green piece down the middle on the WRONG side.

2. Mark off a 2" border on half of one of the back sides and bevel cut a 2" opening following directions in Tools and Techniques chapter. (Diagram 5)

3. Open the frame WRONG side up. Using the tape gun, lay down a layer of double-sided tape on the other (solid) half of the mat, making sure to get close to the edges.

4. Cut a 7" x 7" scrap of fabric. Lay fabric over tape and smooth out. Trim ends with mat knife or rotary cutter.

5. Open the frame tent style. Insert photo. Wrap ribbon around the top of the frame and knot to one side.

6. Add easel.

EASEL

1. On 5 ½" x 6" piece, score as indicated on pattern. You will make the first cut on the WRONG SIDE at 1 ½", flip the board and score on the RIGHT SIDE at 3" and flip over again and score at 4 ½" on the WRONG SIDE.

2. When attaching the easel to the frame section, turn with the RIGHT side up. It should look like the letter "W". Align so easel middle collapses upward into frame. With tape gun, run two lines of tape across the bottom of the frame. Line the easel up even with frame bottom. Press in place. Repeat for other side.

Diagram 5

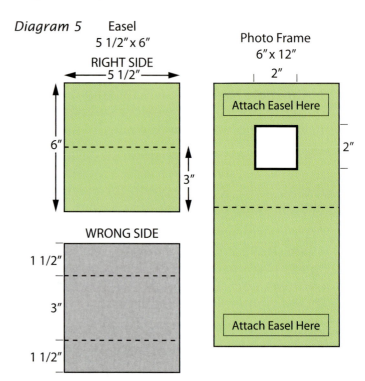

Designer's Tip

Use a piece of sand paper or emery board to sand away any rough spots or jagged edges that may be left. Make sure to check your blade frequently to make sure it's sharp. When you start seeing torn paper on the edge of your board, that's usually the problem! Sanding away the top layer of paper to expose the white board below is also a great way to get that shabby chic look. Rub inks around the edges of the project to distress further. ❧

Make Wedding Memories with Embellishments

Embossed white matboard teams with a cool aqua to lend a trendy yet romantic wedding style. The first project is a unique framed wedding keepsake—a great gift for the lucky couple. A wedding organizer file box helps the bride to keep her wedding on track, and a guest book completes the set.

Time	Difficulty
~3 hrs.	Advanced

Project:

Wedding Keepsake

Technique: Scoring Matboard to Follow a Curve

You will need:

- Crescent # 9225305 embossed white acanthus
- Crescent 1646 sky blue
- 12" x 12" shadow box frame
- Pencil
- Ruler
- Compass
- Patterned paper
- Glue
- White texture paste
- Aqua craft paint to mix in paste
- Glue gun
- Pearls, beads and findings in different sizes, shapes and colors
- Clear beading thread
- Cake decorating bags, tips and accessories
- Tag punch or template

You can create these beautiful, personalized wedding keepsakes that the happy couple will treasure for years to come.

Instructions:

CUT using aqua matboard

- 1 piece to size of back of frame
- 3 ovals, cut in half, in aqua (Diagram 1)

CUT using white embossed board:

- 2 ½" x 5"
- 2 ½" x 7"
- 2 ½" x 9"

1. SCORE on FRONT SIDE of three white boards every ½", creating a long segmented piece of scored board. Fold the two end sections under. On 7" section, punch five evenly spaced, small holes near top to accommodate beading that will be strung on this layer. (Diagram 2)

Diagram 2

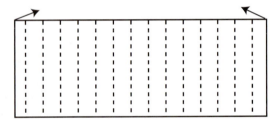

2. Starting on one end, ease rounded part of half oval, RIGHT side up, to inside tops of segmented boards. Repeat with bottom piece. Glue together, giving the cake shape.

3. BOTTOM LAYER: Wrap a 1 ½" length of aqua ribbon around largest layer of cake and knot in the middle front of layer. Trim ends of ribbon.

4. MIDDLE LAYER: Cut an 18" section of invisible beading thread. Knot end and bring through the front left side. Create a desirable pattern of pearls/beads and lay out one section on beading mat. String them on thread. Bring end of thread through the next hole and knot behind. In same hole, bring thread back to front and string another section of beads. Repeat twice more. Knot thread behind final hole and trim. Add additional sequins, flowers, rhinestones or desired trims to fill in gaps where beads end.

Diagram 1

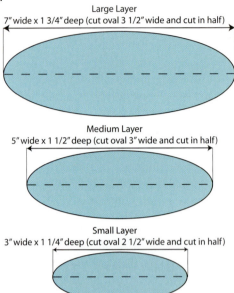

Large Layer
7" wide x 1 3/4" deep (cut oval 3 1/2" wide and cut in half)

Medium Layer
5" wide x 1 1/2" deep (cut oval 3" wide and cut in half)

Small Layer
3" wide x 1 1/4" deep (cut oval 2 1/2" wide and cut in half)

5. TOP LAYER: Add the couple's last initial. The cake in photo has an "H" pin found in a thrift store mounted on a small scrap of matboard. If you don't happen to have something like that, other options including stickers, appliqués, chipboard or wooden letters may be adhered to a scrap of matboard or directly to the cake.

6. In a small bowl, mix a few drops of paint into several tablespoons of texture paste. Stir and add paint until desired frosting color is achieved. Put paste in cake decorating bag. Follow use instructions, replacing "frosting" with "faux frosting!"

7. Ice cake to your liking. If decorating the bottom of the layer, place on wax paper and apply decoration. Allow to dry for several hours. When dry, remove wax paper gently from bottom of cake and add to the stack of layers.

Diagram 3

8. Lay frame on top of matboard and center. Place cake on matboard and lightly mark in pencil lines where cake should go (Diagram 3). When all layers are in place, affix cake to board with glue gun.

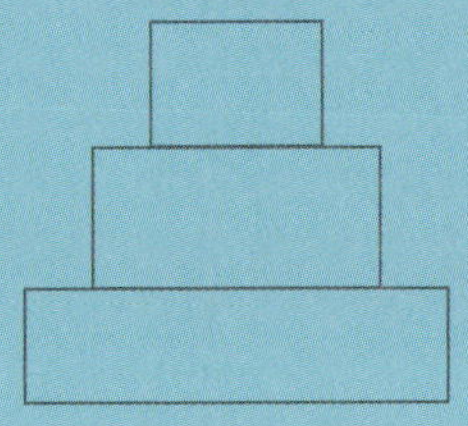

9. Lay frame behind artwork. Draw a light pencil line ½" in from outer edges of the aqua board. Arrange trim to your liking and adhere over mark with quick dry glue. Trim off edges.

10. Print couple's name, date and place of marriage on cardstock and punch out with tag punch. Mount on cardstock and trim. Set eyelets on tags for hanging. Loop ends through ribbon and secure through button shanks. Trim ends of ribbon. Glue in place where desired.

11. Add other touches to the piece that you may have, including wedding invitation or photos. Using glue gun, adhere entire piece to back of frame. Add sawtooth hanger.

Other ideas!

Use the pattern for the wedding cake to celebrate someone's special birthday or a milestone anniversary. Coordinate the colors to suit the occasion—silver for a 25th anniversary or gold for a 50th. Add black candles to the top as a joke for someone going "over the hill," etc. Add memorabilia you have saved to personalize this shadowbox, such as ticket stubs, cards, or concert or show programs. ◈

Designer's Tip

The embossed board does well with stamp inks and chalks. I like to take a stencil brush and brush on my favorite stamp ink color. With the brush, lightly go over the embossed surface. The pattern will stand out more with the soft shading. Or be bold—take the whole stamp pad and press it down directly on the embossed board. The full strength ink will give another look. You can also just ink the edges for another effect. ❧

Time	Difficulty
2 hrs.	Intermediate

Project:

Wedding File Box Organizer

Technique: Box Construction

You will need:

- Crescent # 9225305 white embossed acanthus matboard
- Crescent # 1646 aqua matboard
- Logan 500 Mat Knife
- Heart brads
- Large flat eyelets
- Hole punch tool
- 1 yd. each of two coordinating ribbons
- Scrap paper in coordinating colors
- Square hole punch
- Adhesive foam strips
- 1" magnet tape 16" length
- Tape gun

Instructions:

CUT from white embossed matboard:

- 19 ¾" x 14"
- 9 ¾" x 8"

CUT 12 pieces from aqua matboard

- 9 ½" x 4 ½"
- Cut aqua 5" x 8" for label

Diagram 4
Wedding Organizer Pattern - 9 1/2" x 5" x 4 1/2"
Score on dotted lines. Cut/punch on solid lines.

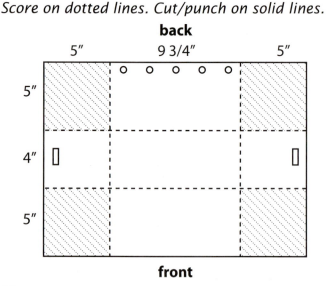

Diagram 5
Wedding Organizer Lid Pattern

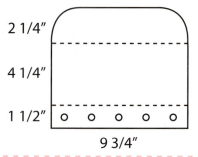

1. Score board on right side referring to pattern. Cut off excess corners (Diagram 4).

2. Trace a curved object (I used a ribbon reel) on the front corners of the lid flaps and trim off with mat knife (Diagram 5).

3. With square punch or mat knife, make slit for ribbon on both sides of box.

4. Mark holes on lid flap. Punch holes. Line up flap with the back of box and mark holes. Punch out.

5. Place lid flap on top of box, matching holes. Use double-sided tape to adhere lid to box. Reinforce with brads or eyelets.

6. Fold up the box and align the sides to meet at 90-degree angles. Run a heavy line of glue up and down inside corners of box where boards meet. Wrap box with several rubber bands to hold in position while glue dries.

7. Cut two pieces of magnet tape 8" each. Place magnet strips on top of each other to ensure they are compatible. Peel backing paper off one and position on front of box, leaving the other magnet attached. Press into place. Carefully close lid. Press sections together (but not TOO hard).

8. Determine the desired length of handle. Cut two lengths of coordinating ribbon. Run a line of double-sided tape down the wrong side of one ribbon. With wrong sides together, carefully adhere ribbons to each other. Cut ends on diagonal.

9. Thread ribbon through slit from inside to outside of box and bring it back out. Punch holes in ribbon with hole punch tool. Insert large eyelet facing out and set. Adjust handle to desired length and bring end of ribbon through the same way as the first and repeat with setting eyelet.

10. For matted label accent, use 5" x 8" aqua piece. First mark 2 ¼" all around WRONG side and bevel cut. Flip mat over to RIGHT side and mark 1 ¾" all around. Bevel cut. (Diagram 6)

11. Print label for organizer on computer. Insert in mat. Wrap ribbon scraps around two corners of the mat. Tape label inside mat. Adhere with four lines of foam mounting tape to box.

File Folder Dividers:

1. On a long strip of 1" wide scrap mat, write the title files for wedding planning. You may want to include: invitations, dress, church, music, photography, florist, programs, budget, reception and miscellaneous.

2. Cut divider titles 1" x length of word. Corners may be rounded with scissors. Place a layer of double-sided tape below the titles. Position title behind each aqua divider and press into place. Arrange them evenly throughout the box.

3. Add # 10 envelopes with bills, receipts, estimates, notes, etc. in the appropriate category.

Diagram 6
Mat Accent for Wedding Organizer

Mark off 2 1/4" and bevel cut WRONG side facing up. Flip to RIGHT side, mark mat at 1 3/4" and bevel cut.

Other ideas!

Before the wedding: Organize your wedding in this small box by dedicating one envelope each to invitations, flowers, church, wedding party, music, photography, and miscellaneous. When you need info, pull out the appropriate envelope and have it close at hand. Make dividers from matboard.

During the wedding: Empty the box and place on a table as your guests come in and they'll be happy to know where to leave their cards and gifts.

After the wedding: Turn the mat dividers over and change your designations to new ones. Label the dividers by month and store your receipts for each month in the box. Or use it for coupons, warranties, recipes, and cancelled checks. ◈

Project:

Guestbook

Time	Difficulty
30 min.	Easy

You will need:

- Crescent # 9225305 white embossed acanthus matboard
- 1/8" hole punch
- Paper for inside of book—lined or scrapbook paper
- White spray paint
- ¾" loose leaf binder rings
- Clip art
- Mat knife
- Aqua dye stamp pad
- Workable Fixative

Instructions:

CUT 2 pieces of white embossed matboard:

- 8 ½" x 8 ½"

CUT about 25 sheets of paper for inside of guest book

- 8" x 8"

1. Rub an aqua dye ink stamp pad over the entire surface of the embossed matboard, making sure to cover all areas equally. Repeat on second board.

2. Mark positions for three holes going down the left side of the white board with which to bind book. Punch holes out of one board. Using that as a pattern, place wrong sides together and punch holes in second board.

3. Spray paint loose leaf binder rings white.

4. Spray both sides of covers with fixative from to seal the cover and protect from rain or messy fingers.

5. Assemble book and join together with painted binder rings. Another option—wrap rings with ribbon and trim ends.

6. Copy the pattern in this book or come up with your own label for the front. Trim the label and mount with foam tape on the front of the guest book. Shade or ink edges with aqua stamp pad if desired.

Technique: Using the Mat Knife

Scissors are great but there is nothing like the control you can get with a good sharp cutting tool. You'll need the Logan Mat Knife with a fresh blade and a piece of glass. Wrap masking tape around the edges of the glass to protect your fingers. The knife will cut many types of materials—paper, Mylar, matboard, acetate and transparencies and photos.

Place item to be trimmed on top of the glass. Start cutting from the top left side of the design and move the design as you go. Make the knife an extension of your arm and keep consistent pressure. Hold the design in place with your non-cutting hand. Move artwork slowly as you cut. Keep your hand straight and don't twist your wrist. Practice following simple shapes and lines.

HINT: Do not drink a big cup of coffee before attempting this. ✍

Other ideas!

This beautiful book will encourage your guests to wax poetic as they inscribe their well wishes on your wedding day. After the wedding, place this book on a table in your entry hall to sign in visitors that you have throughout your married life. Keep a diary of your first year of marriage. Make one in pastels for your friend's new baby and let them record their baby's "first's" (bottle, tooth, lock of hair, steps, etc.). A green and red book can be used to record your Christmas card list or party planning ideas. Use the extra scraps to make place card folders, menu stands, tags, and tiny frames for favors. ◈

Designer's Tip

You will have scrap left over from the various corners and strips trimmed off. This is a fairly expensive board—use up those scraps!

The scraps often come in sets of two or four of the same size, since the outer corners are not used in the designs. It is so quick and easy to make a small book or photo display with these. Bind them with loose leaf rings, punch holes in the sides and tie with ribbon or just take a few binder clips and use them to hold your quick book, photo album or card together. 🌿

Use leftover mat scraps to make place cards like the one shown here.

Deck the Halls with Texture and Embossing

The techniques used in this chapter are nice touches to add to most any paper project. Texturizing with paste adds depth and dimension to a project without distracting from other techniques that may be used at the same time. Dry embossing is so easy and quick, yet adds a subtle twist to a design.

Time	Difficulty
~3 hrs.	Intermediate

Project:

Tree and Gifts Centerpiece

You will need:

- Crescent Shamrock
  - #7111 green suede matboard
  - #1711 black walnut
- Crescent scraps of
  - #9577 stop
  - #SRM3364 green apple
  - #9802 white art
  - #8006 brushed silver
  - #SRM3370 cornflower (colors you have on hand may be substituted)
- Logan Mat knife
- Ruler
- Pencil
- White texture paste
- Glue gun
- Clear bandage tape
- Embellishments for boxes— use what you have!

Instructions for trees:

1. Cut three trees from green suede matboard. (see Diagram 1)

2. Score on lines indicated in patterns (on front side of board), creating three joined triangles. Fold together. Glue inside seams together using a glue gun.

3. Cut three tree trunks from black walnut matboard. Bend on score lines. On WRONG side, run a length of clear bandage tape down one side. Position so two sides meet and press tape in place to secure both ends. Reinforce with glue gun.

4. Place trunk inside tree and glue together.

5. Decorate trees with beads, garland or dab texture paste on as snow or leave plain.

6. Purchase wooden star cut out. Affix toothpick to back of star with glue gun. Dab star with white texture paste on both sides and cover glue and toothpick. Insert star on top of tree through small gap where tree is joined.

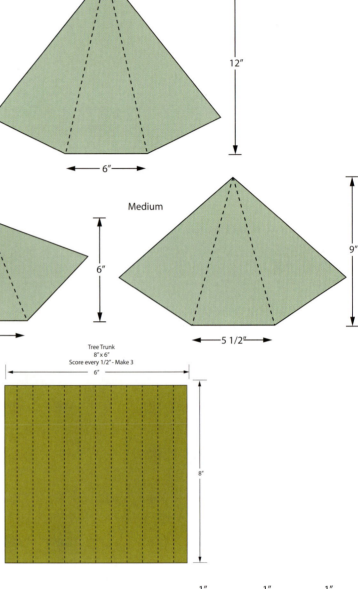

Diagram 1
Large

12"

6"

Medium

9"

Small

6"

5 1/2"

5 1/2"

Tree Trunk
8" x 6"
Score every 1/2" - Make 3

6"

8"

Instructions for packages:

1. Cut 15 boxes in assorted colors—five large, five medium and five small. (Diagram 2)

2. Trim off corners and fold up into box. Decorate boxes before assembling (see Techniques section). Glue corners of boxes and close lids.

3. Place decorated boxes under trees.

4. Set up on holiday table with mirror tiles, faux snow and greenery.

Techniques:

Now you have 15 little boxes! See if you can decorate each one in a unique way. Here are some ideas:

1. Use glitter to highlight the gift boxes. Run a line of glue around the edges of the box and sprinkle with ultra fine or glass glitter.

2. Glue buttons on the lid.

3. Tie up with ribbon or metallic thread.

Diagram 2
*Cut 5 each in
assorted colors*
*Small: 3" x 4"
Medium 6" x 8"
Large: 7" x 8"*

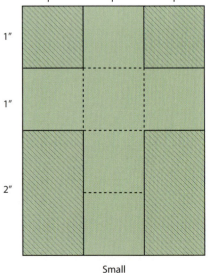

1"   1"   1"

1"

1"

2"

Small
3" x 4"

4. Stamp box with small holiday rubber stamps to decorate.

5. Stencil words of holiday cheer.

6. Doodle a message with markers.

7. Dab on texture paste to look like snow.

8. Add a small piece of greenery and a jingle bell.

9. Punch snowflakes from patterned paper and attach to the top of the box.

10. Place some repositionable reinforcement dots on the box and stencil around them. Remove after painting.

11. Paint a holly leaf on the box.

12. Cover the box with paper and wrap like a present.

13. Add pearls and beads.

14. Accent with metal embellishments.

15. Decorate with stickers.

16. Cover with felt designs.

17. Monogram with initials.

18. Apply a layer of glue or double-sided tape and press microbeads on top to secure.

19. Paint them if you don't have a good selection of scraps on hand.

20. Apply hot fix crystals.

Designer's Tip

If your boxes do not line up exactly, glue them as best you can and wrap with fibers or ribbon. No one will know the difference! Make sure to measure right on the next one. Another way to camouflage a little gap here or there is to fill the space in with texture paste or glue and glitter. This project is an excellent way to practice your box making technique.

Other ideas!

This arrangement may be used as a centerpiece for a holiday meal or party. Then place it on your mantel after the party. Start a new tradition by putting it up each year as one of your favorite decorations. Surround the tree and pile of gifts with heirloom Santas. A string of soft white lights completes the scene.

Use the trees and boxes as an Advent calendar. Make 10 additional boxes and mark each one with a number from 1-25. Put a tiny treasure in each box, a quote from Scripture or your favorite poem. Open one each day as Christmas approaches.

This centerpiece could last all winter if you make additional boxes. On Valentine's Day, use the trees and red and white boxes to set the table for a romantic dinner for two. Wouldn't this be the perfect setting to present your loved one with a special piece of jewelry or engagement ring? Add strands of white berries, hearts and chocolate to add to the table.

For St. Patrick's Day, leave the green boxes under the tree and add some shamrocks and gold coins. Use this centerpiece when you have friends over for corned beef and cabbage!

At Easter time, add pastel eggs, Easter grass and bunnies along with boxes you have already made and see what the Easter bunny thinks... ◈

Project:

Snowman Box

Time	Difficulty
45 min.	Easy

You will need:

- Crescent:
  - Porcelain # 754
  - Raven #1577
- Logan Mat knife
- Clear bandage tape
- Glue gun
- Carrot for nose
- Black snaps or eyelets for eyes and buttons
- Ribbon, fabric or fleece for scarf
- Twigs for arms

Diagram 3

Dimensions for large (12" x 12") box shown. Adjust cut and score lines for medium (9" x 9") and small (6" x 6") boxes

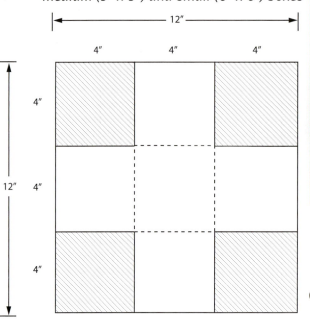

Instructions:

1. Cut three pieces of white board: 6" x 6", 9" x 9" and 12" x 12" (see Diagram 3).

2. Cut two pieces of black: 5" x 5" and 4" x 4".

3. After cutting and scoring three white boards, trim away corners and fold up into boxes. Add decorative trims as desired—eyelets for eyes & buttons, scarf, twigs for arms, and carrot nose. Make sure to do the eyelet setting and other work before folding up the box. If you are using twigs for arms, punch holes where desired. You may want to stabilize the twig arms by inserting a piece of florist's foam snugly inside box. When you insert the twigs, the foam will keep them in place. Glue inside corners to form sturdy box.

4. Place open end of box on top of next larger one and stack from smallest to largest.

5. For hat, cut 5" black square following cutting and scoring directions for box. Fold into box and glue open bottom to 4" black square hat brim.

6. Snowman may be glued together or left separate to stack as nesting boxes for storage.

Other ideas!

Adapt this idea for other seasons: a pile of pumpkins for Halloween, a stack of baby gifts for a shower, a three-tiered wedding cake, you get the idea... and tie the boxes up with a coordinating ribbon. ◈

Designer's Tip

The snowman would be a great addition to your winter centerpiece or he can stand alone. Place him on a mirror tile and add fake snow. Leave sitting on your entryway table to greet visitors as they enter your home. ❦

Time   Difficulty

1 hr.   Intermediate

Project:
Festive Cards and Storage Box

You will need:

- Crescent
  - #SRM3370 Cornflower Blue
- White embossed paper
- Coordinating patterned paper
- Logan:
  - Mat knife
  - Art Deckle 4-Way Stylus
  - Art Deckle ruler
- Ruler
- Pencil
- White texture paste
- Soap
- Brass embossing template—winter theme
- White ink pad
- Small ink dabber
- 1/16" hole punch
- Snowflake brads
- Corner rounder
- 2 pieces of magnet tape 1" x 6"
- Spray adhesive
- Double-sided tape
- Ribbon

Make a set of cards for yourself or as a hostess gift for a handmade reminder of your thoughtfulness.

Instructions:

1. Cut one piece of blue mat 11" x 9 1/2". Cut and score according to pattern (Diagram 4). Cut flap from white embossed paper (Diagram 5).

2. Trim off excess corners.

3. Place brass stencil where artwork is desired. Make sure it is facing the right direction once box is assembled.

4. With embossing stylus, press tip firmly into openings of template. You may need a smaller stylus tip depending on the pattern. Make sure all lines in the design are embossed and remove stencil.

5. Load ink dabber with white ink and lightly swirl ink over where you have just embossed. The ink will stay on the surface and the embossed lines will be more visible.

6. See tips on next page to make your own double sided paper. Cut paper for flap.

7. Mark position of brads on inside of box and punch small holes. Lay box on flap as a guide and pencil in where holes should go. Punch holes. Lay a line of double-sided tape down the length of the box flap. Lay paper on top

of flap, lining up holes. Press down to secure. Set brads so snowflake is on the outside top of the box.

8. Punch rectangular hole in top sides of box for ribbon handle. Cut length of ribbon and thread through openings. Lay a 7" line of tape down the back middle of the ribbon. Adhere ribbon to top flap of box, covering backs of brads. Pull ribbon through holes in sides and tie on the outside.

9. Cut two 6" strips of magnet tape and face magnetic sides together. Peel off one layer of adhesive and place magnet where desired. Remove backing from the other piece of magnet and carefully line up where desired. Press in place.

Instructions for cards:

1. Cut white textured cardstock 7" x 10" and fold in half to create a 5" x 7" card. With Logan Art Deckle ruler, tear ½" off bottom of card. Ink edges with blue ink.

2. Cut a 4" x 6" piece of patterned paper. Position and center brass template on patterned paper. With flat knife, spread white texture paste over stencil making sure to cover all openings. Carefully lift stencil off and allow to dry for 1 hour.

3. Write message in pencil at bottom of card. Adhere to white card with tape gun.

4. Make a set for everyone! When set is complete, tie with matching ribbon.

Designer's Tip

Before pressing down through stencil, rub tip of stylus in soap to allow stylus to glide over matboard.

Double-sided patterned paper is not always available in the color and texture you'd like. Not a problem—you can make your own! Simply select the two papers you'd like. Spray wrong sides of both papers with spray adhesive. Carefully align them and press together. Voila! Double-sided paper!

Diagram 4

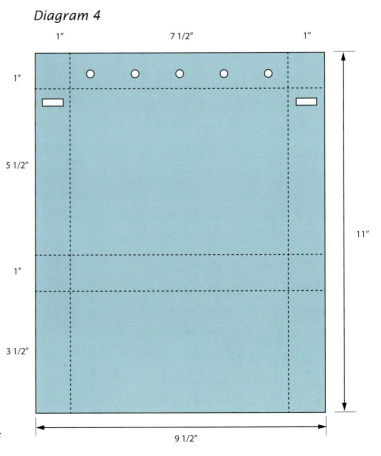

Diagram 5

Holiday Card Box Lid
7 1/5" x 4"

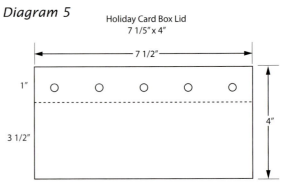

Other ideas!

Cards are not just for Christmas or holidays. Get a stack of supplies, set aside an evening and make birthday gifts for all of your friends and family. Who doesn't appreciate personalized handmade cards in a beautiful box to match?

Make a set in school colors for your son or daughter going off to college. Include an address book with all of their family addresses, emails and phone numbers. Don't forget to include stamps and return address labels. This may increase your chance of hearing from them!

Matboard as Art

The traditional function of matting is to surround artwork with empty space allowing the viewer's eye to focus and come to rest on what lies inside the window.

Although it is very tempting to embellish with all of the fun supplies available these days, a little restraint should be shown when decorating mats. It's very easy to take out the stamp pad and decorate every square inch. Often, the mat can be prettier than the artwork! But sometimes you need to give your eyes a rest and allow them to take in the beauty of a simple photograph of a flower, a child's face, or a crayon drawing created for you by your little one. Just keep it in mind...

Certainly, a mat cutter is the optimum choice for working on any of the projects in the book, but most of them can be accomplished with careful measurement, a T-square, pencil, cork-backed metal ruler (cork backing prevents the ruler from slipping when pressure is applied), and a sharp mat knife.

For in-depth instruction on mat cutting, I recommend reading, "Basic Mat Cutting" by Vivian C. Kistler. There is also a very good DVD available which demonstrates the use of the Logan system step by step. It is included with the 301-S Compact Mat Cutting kit. 🖌

Matboard is more than just a border in this chapter! Framed art goes 3-D in these fun and decorative wall hanging projects.

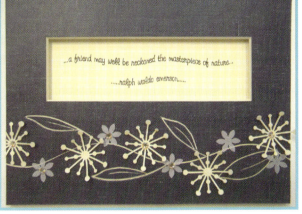

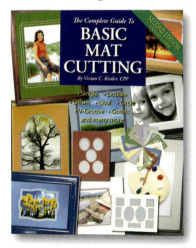

Project:
Photo Mosaic

Time	Difficulty
1.5 hrs.	Intermediate

Diagram 1

2 1/2"

16"

As your family expands, you can easily update this photo collage with the newest members' pictures. This project is a great way to use small amounts of leftover matboard!

You will need:

- Crescent
    - # 9908 Cambridge for outside mat (16" x 16") and artwork base (18" x 18")
- 36 pieces of scrap board in various colors cut into 1 ½" squares
- Logan:
    - Mat knife
    - 301-S Mat Cutter
- 16" x 16" frame without glass
- Spray paint
- Foam tape
- Tape gun
- Spray adhesive
- Black and white photos cropped and sized to 1 ½"

Instructions:

CUT Matboard as indicated above.

Spray paint frame if desired.

1. On 18" square board, score 1" on all sides on the WRONG side. Make sure to measure the rabbet, or inside recess of the frame, very carefully and work from that measurement.

2. Trim off excess corners and bend 1" borders up 90 degrees to form a shadow box.

3. With 16" square mat, measure and mark a 2 ½" border all around on the WRONG side and bevel cut the mat. Follow directions in Tools and Techniques section.

4. Lay the 2 ½" beveled mat inside of the background. Lightly pencil marks to show boundaries where the artwork should be contained.

5. Cut the piece of fallout from the beveled mat down to 10" x 10". Start laying tiles out on the fallout in a pleasing arrangement. Place the tiles next to each other leaving about 1/8" or so in between tiles. Intersperse the photos throughout the design.

6. When you have an arrangement that you like, add foam tape to the back of each tile and press into place. On each photo tile, add two layers of foam tape. This will give dimension to the arrangement. When tile composition is complete, adhere foam tape strips to back of 10" x 10" tiled piece.

7. Remove adhesive strips. Place tiled section into penciled marks. When lined up squarely, press down to secure to backing board.

8. Place beveled mat, then shadow box section into frame. With masking tape, secure background board to frame.

9. Place on easel to display or add eye hooks and wire on the back sides of frame and hang!

Designer's Tip

I found this frame at a thrift store for $1. Often you can find really good deals on beautiful frames that are just missing the glass. Snap them up when you see them and use them to display dimensional artwork. With a quick coat of spray paint, you have a fresh new masterpiece. Buy several and paint them the same color and you have a whole new wall arrangement!

Frame your children's first pair of shoes, an old sterling silver spoon or a piece of vintage clothing or lace. Make sure to use the right adhesive for the job. Because you are not restricted by having to stay inside the glass, anything goes!

Techniques: Retroframing

Retroframing is a process of fitting artwork into a frame you already have. Matting is the medium that blends the two disparate pieces into one cohesive piece of art. Of course, a few conditions must be met:

1. The artwork must be smaller than the frame.

2. You must have a good attitude, probably some spray paint and a bit of creativity.

3. Accept that if it doesn't work out, at least it was a good try and you probably learned what not to do the next time.

Choose matboard that works with the art and the frame, if that is possible. If that is not happening, the easiest thing to change is the color of the frame, since the artwork is the main focus, not the frame. I recommend matting to complement the artwork, not the room it will be hung in. The matted and framed artwork should stand on its own wherever it is placed. However, a safe choice for frame or mat color is white, off-white or black. It's hard to go wrong with that. But if you really want the artwork to pop, be brave and mat in color. Don't discount colors until you put the mat up

to the artwork and try it. You will know when you see what you like. Go for it!

OK, so let's do this... The measurements given are for the frame used in the design. Feel free to change them to accommodate the frame you are working with. Starting with the outer frame measurements, work your way in to the middle. For example, in the sample, the rabbet measures 16" square.

For a frame that size, a 2 1/2" to 3" border surrounding the artwork is recommended. Anything less would be out of proportion and look insignificant. (However, you could go wider for a cool effect. A very large border draws your attention to the artwork contained within, making it appear prominent and of value.)

Going with a 2 ½" border all around, the area available for your artwork is 11" (16" outside minus 2 ½" border x 2 [each side] = 5), and 16 minus 5= 11"). In that 11", you need to leave room in between tiles and a little more between mat and tiles. I like the look of 6 tiles going across and down. 11" divided by 6 = 1 7/8" so if the tile is cut 1 ½", that's plenty of room left over for the borders.

Other ideas!

Using the technique described in the photo mosaic project, show the progress of your child's growth from kindergarten to 8th grade. Or fill with photos of your child's friends. Maybe you don't live near family—take pictures the next time you are home, insert their photos in a frame like this and play "Who is this relative?" with your children. All will be delighted at the next visit when the kids recognize Aunt Catherine and Cousin Bobby!

Consider matting collections in the same color to visually group them and really pack a punch. Some items, beyond the traditional artwork, photographs and needlework, that may be matted are: coins, military ribbons and medals, stamps, matchbooks, ticket stubs, bottle caps, shells, quilt blocks, silverware, and dried flowers.

Every year at the holidays, I create matted postage stamp ornaments using the holiday stamp for that year. On the back is a short recap of what's been happening at our house in the last year. So it's a card, ornament and letter all in one! It's also nice to go into the homes of our friends and family and see the series of our family's ornaments hanging on their Christmas tree. ◈

Techniques: Mats and frames

In selecting items to mat, think about whether you will be framing with or without glass. Objects that will surpass the height of one or two layers of a mat window (about 1/8") will push against the glass or cause the backing board to bow out. Such a piece will need either to be recessed (as in a shadow box) or framed without glass. A frame without glass will require dusting and may not be practical for items of value, leaving them open to damage, such as moisture or dirt. Place pieces out of direct sunlight as anything will fade when exposed to this.

Artwork can be framed professionally or quite inexpensively... if you are willing to work a little. Many frames in good condition may be found at thrift stores, garage sales or in your own home. A coat of paint is often all that is required to give new life to an outdated frame. Dents and scratches can be sanded out and a new color sprayed on in a matter of minutes. If you are lucky enough to find a nice custom wood frame without glass for a few dollars, it's still well worth a small investment for custom cut glass. Standard size glass can also be purchased at craft stores.

I like to spray paint larger frames in my latest favorite color and hang them on the wall. Inside I place smaller photos and mementos for a wall arrangement. Or corkboard could be

inserted, backed with foam core and used as a bulletin board.

Another really inexpensive (notice I'm trying not to use the word cheap because that implies low quality, which this is not) way to frame is by using clear acrylic box frames.

Create your own shadowbox by measuring the exact dimensions of the inside of the box frame. Score matboard along all four sides the same depth as the frame. Cut on the wrong side so the color appears on the inside and then mat 3D objects inside. Use to frame a graduating senior's tassel or a baby spoon birth announcement for a new baby. Acrylic is prone to scratch easily, so normally I buy them new as opposed to secondhand. A plastic saw tooth tab hanger is all that is needed to hang the project as long as it's fairly light. Keep your eyes out and pick up a few frames when you see a good deal. With a little planning, you can usually mat creatively and fit the artwork to the frame.

Once you get the hang of cutting mats, you will always be anticipating your next project. When you have all the supplies right there at your fingertips, it's so quick and easy to pick up a project, mat it, frame it and hang it in an evening. I have saved my family many dollars in the gift department. And everyone appreciates a handmade or personalized present. ◈

Project:
Baby Collage

Time	Difficulty
2 hrs.	Easy

You will need:

- 11" x 14" frame with glass
- Crescent # 1577 raven black
- Color photos
- Text created by computer, by hand or digitally inserted into photos
- Spray adhesive
- Sandpaper
- Foam tape
- Embellishments—metal, paper punches, eyelets
- Eyelet setter
- Hole punch
- Glue
- Tape gun

Instructions:

1. Select photos you would like to use in layout.

2. On 11" x 14" black matboard, lay the photos out in an arrangement that you like. Allow about ¼" to ½" additional around each photo for mat border. Select three or four background colors that blend well with the photos. Using spray adhesive on the back of the photos, mat on scrap mat in desired colors, leaving a small border of color behind photo.

3. Position photos on black mat. At this point, determine whether you would like to add additional embellishments, such as text/journaling, title, memorabilia, eyelets, punches or stickers. If so, figure out where you want them in the layout.

4. With foam tape, adhere photos where you'd like them.

5. Fill in with other items as desired and adhere to backing. (If you are adding eyelets or

Using digital photos, you can add text onto your images before printing them.

anything dimensional, you will probably want to do that before the photos are put on to allow room to work).

6. Make sure all artwork is the same height when you lay it in the frame.

7. Clean glass and insert in frame. Lay photo board into frame and place backing board behind. Staple or use framers points to secure back of frame. Finish back with backing paper and add saw tooth hanger on back.

Designer's Tip

The time spent measuring to cut actual beveled windows for a finished piece like this would take forever! You get almost the same effect in a lot less time by matting each photo on a background color and mounting it on top of the backing board. The black background gives depth to the arrangement. I inked the edges of each backing mat white for a further illusion of depth.

For a less formal layout, turn the photos at angles to each other. This arrangement does take up a little more room but less time to line up. Feel free to add embellishments and journaling that help to tell the story of your design. 🌿

Matboard makes a great surface for scrapping pages. Why not hang your pages on the wall for all to enjoy?

Other ideas!

This project is fun because you can put it together very quickly. With photos, a frame, embellishments on hand and a little time to yourself, you could whip up one of these in no time.

Some ideas for themes might include: first day of school, first year of life, birthday parties (young and old), retirement celebrations, fun at the beach, military ceremonies, family gatherings at Thanksgiving (think about it—there are your family's gifts for Christmas!),

holiday cookie exchanges, your special pet, memories of a loved one, or any event you want to remember.

A framed collage of the seaside town in NJ would be a perfect thank you for the friends who lent you their beach house for a weekend getaway. There are many people who do nice things for us. Use your creativity and take some time to thank them in return for their kindnesses—it means so much more than a gift card! ◈

Project:
Groovy Friend

Time   Difficulty

1.5 hrs.   Intermediate

You will need:

- Logan 301-S and bevel cutting head
- Logan Groovy Mouse
- Crescent #4851
- Flower punches (medium and small)
- Scrapbook paper/vellum
- Glue
- Double-sided tape
- Foam board scraps
- Quote lettered by computer or hand to fit in window of mat
- Embellishments (I used flat backed crystals)

Instructions:

1. Cut denim matboard to 5" x 7".

2. Cut an opening measuring 1 ½" x 5". See Diagram 2.

3. Follow directions for use of the Groovy Mouse. Freehand cut a gently curving line for the vine. Carefully line up the mouse and cut leaves along the vines. If you are feeling especially adventurous, cut some veins in the leaves.

4. From foam board scraps, trim strips:

   2 measuring ¾" x 4 ½"

   1 measuring ¾" x 5"

   1 measuring 2" x 5"

5 Apply double-sided tape with tape gun to the back of the mat. Place foam board strips on back of mat.

6. Print quote. Center in the window and adhere to back of mat behind foam board.

7. Punch flowers from scrapbook paper in coordinating colors. Glue on to the mat filling in spaces where there are no leaves. Glue accent to the flower centers—a bead, mirror,

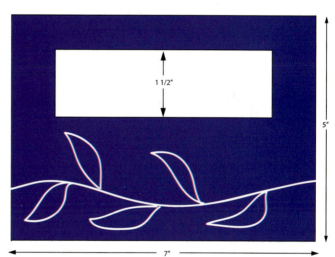

Diagram 2

glitter, crystal, eyelet or button, as desired.

8. This mat may be framed or an easel backing can be added to stand it up.

Use foam board scraps to elevate the matboard for extra dimension. Adhere the scraps to the back using the tape gun.

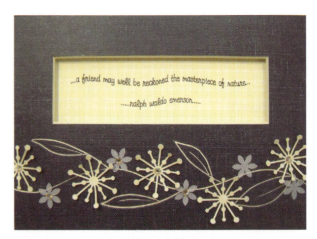

Add die cuts, beads and other embellishments, or whatever else you have on hand. Use your imagination and resourcefulness for a custom look.

Designer Tips: On dust covers

You may not think this is important, but to me, a finished back perfectly completes the piece you have framed. When I'm done matting and framing a piece, I add a dust cover to the back. This not only looks professional but it protects artwork from dust, smoke, or whatever else is floating around in the air that can degrade your artwork!

There are a few ways to do this. The following was the first method I learned. It's a little messy but finishes nicely. Thoroughly wet a piece of brown kraft paper (like a paper bag) cut about an inch larger all around than the frame. Run a line of glue along the back of the frame. Place the paper on top, smoothing out any air bubbles, and let it dry. Trim the edges off by turning the frame over and carefully running a mat knife right along the frame edge. Cut on a self-healing mat of course! The paper will dry tight to the frame back.

The other method I use is a little quicker.

Trim the paper down to just a little smaller than the frame. Run a line of double-sided tape close to the outer edge of the frame back. Lay the paper on one end of the frame back and ease and smooth paper down the rest of the frame. Trim excess paper if necessary.

Honestly, brown kraft paper? Boring! There are so many colorful papers available that work just as well and look a lot nicer. Wallpaper is a good

choice because it's heavy and comes in the perfect width for most items I frame. For larger pieces, I use sturdy gift wrap. You can recycle old calendars, cards, gift bags or posters. Scrapbooking paper is great for this too. Allover prints are easier to work with than stripes, checks or anything with straight lines in them.

I like to tie in the backing to the framed artwork. For example, a birth announcement might feature pink ticking wallpaper on the back, a wedding watercolor uses some beautiful embossed gift wrap, candy cane wrapping paper backing matted Christmas photo ornaments…

You get the idea- be creative and use what you have on hand. You'll be surprised what you come up with.

The dust cover is also where I write my message to the recipient. If the piece is one I have done for hire, a label with my contact information is included.

Saw tooth hangers that nail directly into the frame are my choice for hanging small pieces of artwork. The larger and heavier pieces can be hung by attaching two screw eyes to the sides of the frame about 1/3 of the way down from the top. Take a length of picture hanging wire and thread through both screw eyes several times, keeping wire fairly taut. Twist wire together to finish. Wire should not be seen from the front of the frame. ❦

Other ideas!

The Groovy Mouse is a great tool from Logan. What it does is cut a v-groove into your matboard. There are a few ways you can use it. The mouse has a slot on the side so you can slip it over the guide rail of the mat cutter, engage the blade and pull down for a perfectly straight cut. OR you can freehand cut whatever design you like. Another option is to combine the two—first, freehand cut a design and then use the straight cutter to enclose the design with a border cut. Gentle curves and lines work best but after a little practice you will want to experiment further. Make sure to read the instructions before use—those blades are SHARP! Take some time to work with this tool and see all the possibilities. I like using this technique and adding accents. That way, if the leaf I cut is less than perfect, I can hide the mistake with a flower or other embellishment. And the point of doing all this is to have fun, right? No pressure...

Is that groovy or what?

Above: The Logan Groovy Mouse, and sample mats showing the variety of styles possible with this groovy tool. Below: Design possibilities with Groovy Mouse...courtesy of Logan Graphic Products.

Victorian House

This project started out as a three-dimensional house with a roof and sides. I was on my way to a trade show and wanted to present this as a "Get to know me" piece of art for my display. However, at 2 AM the night before we were leaving for the show, I realized it wasn't going to happen. So I thought if I made it to fit in a frame, it would be easier to transport and quicker to finish!

I started to work by cutting the shape of the house and window openings for the basic shape from matboard. The photo of my family that spans the first floor was cut into three sections so the people fit behind each window. (I am in the doorway saying hi!) The windows were made from clear styrene.

The most fun part was adding all of the little touches like the window boxes, shutters, scalloped roof gingerbread and beaded roof line and door knob. The sun, star, flowers and wreath were punched from cardstock using paper punches. The background was made by using my Logan bevel cutter freehand to make some rolling hills. For the fence posts, I used the straight cutter and chopped ½" fence posts and trimmed the top into a point with scissors. The three dimensional effect for the piece is achieved by adding layers of foam core in between to give dimension. The stairs were added at the end for a finishing touch.

The frame was one I happened to have on hand. So before I started I knew everything would have to fit into an 11" x 14" opening.

Although this project didn't turn out as I'd planned, I really like the finished product. Did I mention I am one who works best under pressure? As the sign in the window says, *"Welcome to my world!"*

Right: Use embossed matboard to construct your own scrapbook covers or pocket folders. Here watercolors are used to add color enhancements.

Ideas for Inspiration

N ow that you understand basic matboard construction techniques, let your own imagination inspire you! Here are more ideas that build on the cutting, joining, and embellishing techniques described in previous chapters. Almost anything you can imagine you can build with matboard. So get inspired and build something to enhance your home or give as a gift. **Author's warning: this is a seriously addictive hobby!**

Holiday Card Gift Box, Beach Themed Storage Boxes and Photo Album

No baking required for these beautiful creations! Using matboard with beads, texture paste, stencils and other embellshments, these projects make a great centerpiece or display.

At left: a silverware box headed for the trash is repurposed as a bead box. Enhanced with matboard cut-outs on the lid, plus beads and ribbon around the rim.

At right: Another cute idea for a desk set, including blotter with tied-on important phone numbers (simply replace the tag when the numbers change), plus memo notepad holder, pen caddy and decorative note holder.

At left: Mat board is stamped and scored to create this attractive and useful note holder. Hang one on the refrigerator or near the phone for those important lists and messages.

More fun ideas! Clockwise from the top: Another folder idea, Locker organizer, and monogrammed memory box.

Clockwise from top: Clever matboard layering creates this framed holiday door art; CD covers for storage or as gift wrap; Another spin on the holiday card box theme shown here with embossed snowmen.

Conclusion

hope you have found something in this book that you can use on your creative journey. Even for someone who has never worked with any of these tools, most of the projects are very easy to construct. With a little patience and practice, you can be designing projects of your own. I can't stress enough that once you learn the basics of mat cutting and become familiar with the tools, you will be free to make whatever you want! The projects in this book are just a small sample of what can be done and hopefully will give you ideas to start with.

If you are a card maker, a box to put your handmade cards in is a great project to start with. For scrap bookers, a matted and framed layout is a perfect showcase for that page that you spent five hours working on.

Whatever your background or skill, I hope that you will give the techniques described in this book a try. I can only say that I have spent many happy hours in my studio cutting, scoring and embellishing. The tools and supplies available today are amazing. I don't know about you but I have a lot of gadgets, paper, beads, glitter, stamps, punches and paint. When there is an opportunity to use them on quick and fun projects, I'm so happy to have them on hand and find the perfect place to add them.

Thanks for reading and happy crafting!

Sources

Here is a list of my preferred products and their suppliers.

Foam Tape Strips

Therm O Web Adhesives

- Sticky Strips® Foam Tape

770 Glenn Avenue
Wheeling, IL 60090
ph. 847-520-5200
www.ThermoWeb.com

Glitter

Art Institute Glitter, Inc.™

- Vintage Glass Glitter (used on gift boxes in Deck the Halls, Chapter 5)

www.artglitter.com

Glue

Beacon Adhesives

- Zip Dry Paper Glue

Customer Service: 1-800-865-7238
www.beaconcreates.com

Mat Cutting Tools

Logan Graphic Products, Inc.

- 301-S Compact Mat Cutter with straight and bevel cutting heads
- A1303 Art Deckle 4-Way Stylus
- 500 Mat Knife
- 707 Groovy Mouse

1100 Brown Street
Wauconda, IL 60084 USA
ph. 847-526-5515
toll free 800-331-6232
www.logangraphic.com

Matboard

Crescent® Cardboard Company, Inc.

www.crescentcardboard.com

Paper

Die Cuts With A View

www.diecutswithaview.com

Ribbon

Berwick Offray LLC

For a complete list of retailers, visit:

www.Offray.com

Spray Finishes

Krylon®

- Krylon® Workable Fixatif

  Used throughout the book to set chalks, markers and computer printed surfaces to prevent smudging when touched

- Krylon® Spray Adhesive

  Used throughout the book to adhere paper to paper

- Krylon® Interior-Exterior Paint- Almond #1506

  Paint used on frame in the jewelry wall hanger

- Krylon® Preserve It!®

  Protect projects being handled from dirt, oils, moisture in desk set and throughout book

- Krylon® Matte Finish

  Spray on any project that will be used on a regular basis to protect from the elements and everyday wear and tear to extend the life of the item

www.Krylon.com
1-800-4KRYLON
(1-800-457-9566)

Stamping Supplies

Tsukineko®

- VersaMark® Ink (used in Desk Set chapter to stamp flowers)

www.tsukineko.com

Stencil Supplies

Dreamweaver Stencils

- Embossing paste (used in Wedding chapter to ice cake)

1335 Cindee Lane
Colton, CA 92324
Phone: 909-824-8343
Email: lynell@abac.com
www.dreamweaverstencils.com

Threads, Decorative

Kreinik Mfg. Co., Inc.

- Metallic threads (used in Holiday chapter to wrap matboard boxes)

1-800-537-2166
www.kreinik.com

Logan Graphic Products is proud to offer a wide variety of tools for the artist and hobbyist.
Mat, Frame, Finish, Enhance *and* **Learn** *with Logan.*
Please visit our website for a dealer near you:
www.logangraphic.com

Mat

3-STEP OVAL & CIRCLE MAT CUTTER

3-Step Oval and Circle Mat Cutter is easy to use, fast and portable. Cuts ovals or circles on the surface of the matboard using a patented 3-step mechanism for gradual increase of blade depth.

Converts from oval to circle cutter with a turn of a knob. Ovals from 3 1/4" x 4 3/4" to 20" x 23". Circles from 4 1/2" to 20".

3-Step Oval & Circle Mat Cutter - Model 201
Replacement Blade #324

ARTIST'S V-GROOVER AND COMPACT V-GROOVER ADAPTER

Simplex V-Groover offers a way to cut surface V-Grooves quickly and accurately with zero overcuts.

Push-Pull action cuts V-Grooves right on the surface of the matboard, eliminating any need for trimming or taping. Works entirely with stops. Can also work on Compact mat cutter by adding the #303 Compact V-Groove Adapter.

Artist's V-Groover - Model 703

Compact V-Groover Adapter - Model 303

Replacement Blade #1258

GROOVY MOUSE

Groovy Mouse ™ cuts decorative V-grooves onto mat surfaces. Use it freestyle or with most Logan rail systems. Groovy Mouse can also be used to cut freeform mat openings. Featuring a unique swirl pattern and ergonomic design, Groovy Mouse also houses a convenient blade storage compartment. Includes two V-Groove replacement blades and one snip-off blade, plus a handy corner marking tool. Get your V-Groove on with Groovy Mouse!

Groovy Mouse #707

Replacement Blade Kit #326

450 INTERMEDIATE +
40" Board mounted mat cutting system with parallel mat guide, 90 degree squaring bar, colored board surface, hinged guide rail with production stop and straight and bevel cutting heads. Includes creative matting instructions and five extra blades. Plus FREE set up and instruction DVD.

Replacement Blade #270

INCLUDES SET-UP & INSTRUCTIONAL DVD

750 SIMPLEX PLUS
40" base board with high pressure laminate surface, hinged guide rail with scaled production stops, mat guide in aluminum channels, 27" squaring arm, plus straight and bevel cutting heads. Free set up DVD included. Also available in 60" version as model #760.

Replacement Blade #270

INCLUDES SET-UP & INSTRUCTIONAL DVD

650 FRAMER'S EDGE
40" board cutter with high pressure laminate surface, hinged guide rail with scaled production stop, movable head production stop, mat guide in aluminum channels, 27" squaring arm, plus dual purpose straight and bevel cutting head. Free set up DVD included. Also available in 48" version as model #655. 60" version is model #660.

Replacement Blade #269

INCLUDES SET-UP & INSTRUCTIONAL DVD

Frame

PRO SAW

Custom engineered for precise miter cuts. Has multiple angle settings and cuts up to 2.5" moulding with a superfine 24 TPI saw blade for clean cuts. Includes two secure hold clamps with a 36" left and 18" right scaled fence.

Pro Saw - Model F100-2

PRECISION SANDER

10 lb. wheel that sands up to 2.5" moulding. Sands to improve saw cut miters to perfect 45° along with 5-, 6-, and 8-sided frames.

Precision Sander - Model F200-1

STUDIO JOINER

Drives all V-Nail sizes on a magnetic nail holder. Quick depth adjustment, can be used on hard or soft woods. Use on mouldings up to 2.5".

Studio Joiner - Model F300-1

PRO JOINER

Patent pending V-Nail alignment pins. Adjustable nail spacing guide and settings. Drives all nail sizes and can be used for stacking nails. Use on mouldings up to 2.5", in soft or hard wood.

Pro Joiner - Model F300-2

FRAME SHOP IN A BOX KIT

Complete set of framing tools including Pro Saw, Precision Sander, Studio Joiner and Fitting Tool. Kit includes enough practice wood moulding to create an 11x14 frame, plus has an 11x14 pre-cut mat, 11x14 foamboard backing and hanging hardware to complete your first frame. Also includes a copy of the F245 book.

Frame Shop in a Box - Model F600-A

Finish

FITTING TOOL

Unique patented rotating head design drives and removes four different inserts. No slipping or bending. Use on hard or soft wood and drives inserts into moulding up to 2.5".

Fitting Tool - Model 400-1

DUAL DRIVE POINT DRIVER

Production level insert gun that uses stacked points of either rigid or flexible inserts. Features a tension adjustment to use on either hard or soft wood moulding.

Dual Drive Point Driver - Model F500-1

Enhance

Art Deckle tools and accessories let you create custom embossed patterns and deckled edges on most types of paper. Art Deckle is a fantastic set of tools for creative custom greeting cards, invitations, and scrapbook pages.

ART DECKLE DECKLING TOOLS

With Art Deckle, it's easy to make a perfect decorative deckled edge. Constructed of ultra-thin, hardened stainless steel with a non-repeating natural deckle edge. There is even a 36" (91cm) version big enough to deckle full sheets of watercolor paper.

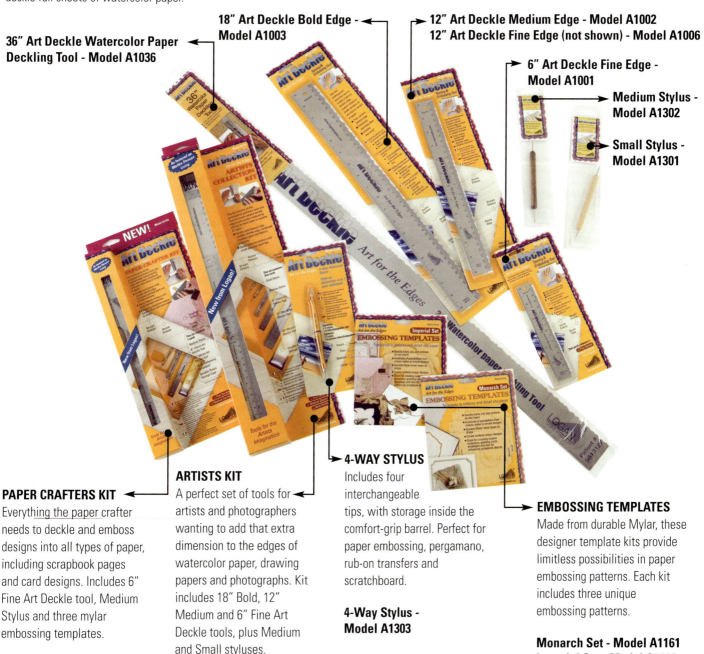

36" Art Deckle Watercolor Paper Deckling Tool - Model A1036

18" Art Deckle Bold Edge - Model A1003

12" Art Deckle Medium Edge - Model A1002
12" Art Deckle Fine Edge (not shown) - Model A1006

6" Art Deckle Fine Edge - Model A1001

Medium Stylus - Model A1302

Small Stylus - Model A1301

PAPER CRAFTERS KIT
Everything the paper crafter needs to deckle and emboss designs into all types of paper, including scrapbook pages and card designs. Includes 6" Fine Art Deckle tool, Medium Stylus and three mylar embossing templates.

Paper Crafters Kit - Model A1170

ARTISTS KIT
A perfect set of tools for artists and photographers wanting to add that extra dimension to the edges of watercolor paper, drawing papers and photographs. Kit includes 18" Bold, 12" Medium and 6" Fine Art Deckle tools, plus Medium and Small styluses.

Artists Kit - Model A1171

4-WAY STYLUS
Includes four interchangeable tips, with storage inside the comfort-grip barrel. Perfect for paper embossing, pergamano, rub-on transfers and scratchboard.

4-Way Stylus - Model A1303

EMBOSSING TEMPLATES
Made from durable Mylar, these designer template kits provide limitless possibilities in paper embossing patterns. Each kit includes three unique embossing patterns.

Monarch Set - Model A1161
Imperial Set - Model A1162

Learn

To learn where to buy other great Logan products, view hints & tips, locations of classes and free demonstrations on-line, visit us at **www.logangraphic.com**

Also available are 3 different books on matting and framing by Vivian C. Kistler, CPF. Each book is 64 pages.

Available through Logan dealers

Basic Mat Cutting - Model 238
Mat Decoration Book- Model 240
Do It Yourself Picture Framing- Model 241

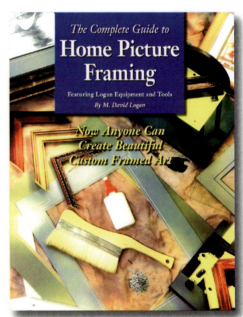

LOGAN®
GRAPHIC PRODUCTS, INC.
Tools for Art - Tools for Life

www.logangraphic.com

Logan Graphic Products, Inc.
1100 Brown Street
Wauconda, IL 60084 USA

Phone (847) 526-5515

Fax (847) 526-5155

Toll Free (800) 331-6232

info@logangraphic.com

For more creative ideas in matting, pick up a copy of Logan's **"How To Cut Mats"** DVD by Vivian C. Kistler, CPF. - **Model 237D**

Available through Logan dealers.

Complete and detailed directions featuring Logan's picture framing tools system. Learn inside secrets from professional framers for creating your own custom framed art. 92 pages.

Home Picture Framing - Model F245